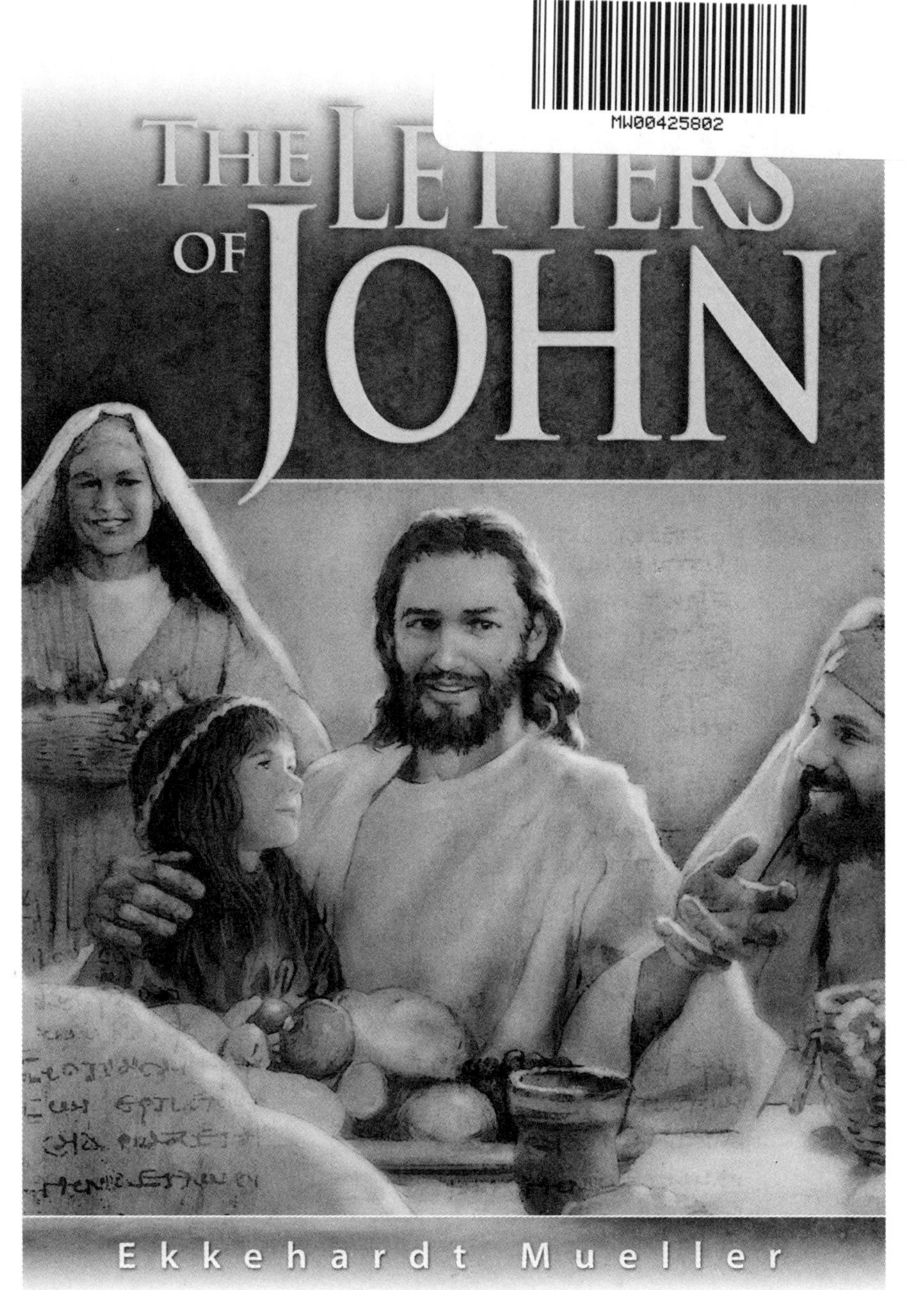

Pacific Press® Publishing Association
Nampa, Idaho
Oshawa, Ontario, Canada
www.pacificpress.com

Cover design by Gerald Lee Monks
Cover design resources from Lars Justinen
Inside design by Aaron Troia

Unless otherwise noted, Bible translations are the author's own.

You can obtain additional copies of this book by calling toll-free 1-800-765-6955 or by visiting http://www.adventistbookcenter.com.

Library of Congress Cataloging-in-Publication Data

Mueller, Ekkehardt, 1950-
The letters of John / Ekkehardt Mueller.
p. cm.
ISBN 13: 978-0-8163-2333-3 (paperback)
ISBN 10: 0-8163-2333-X (paperback)
1. Bible. N.T. Epistles of John—Commentaries. I. Title.
BS2805.53.M84 2009
227'.94077—dc22

2008053013

09 10 11 12 13 • 5 4 3 2 1

Third Quarter 2009

DEDICATION

Lovingly dedicated to Geri,
my wonderful wife and best friend

TABLE OF CONTENTS

CHAPTER 1

JESUS AND THE JOHANNINE LETTERS

Life is filled with much tension, friction, and conflict, isn't it? This is true of international politics, economics, our personal lives, and religion. Even within Christianity, there are heretical views, political power plays, and sometimes even violence.

John had to face such a situation in the first century A.D. The churches to which he wrote suffered from theological conflicts, especially concerning the nature of Jesus. These theological dissensions had practical implications for Christian lifestyle. John had to address problematic teachings, wrong behavior, and a power struggle within his churches.

I. From Whom and to Whom: Author and Recipients

The three letters of John are found toward the end of the New Testament canon. The first is not addressed to any specific church. First John is comparable in size to other New Testament letters. However, 2 John and 3 John belong among the four New Testament epistles that consist of one chapter only and are the shortest in the New Testament.

The first epistle begins by presenting the Word of life. It contains no formal introduction, nor a real conclusion. The author does not introduce himself, nor does he inform us about his audience. The second and third letters mention "the elder" and tell us to whom they are addressed.

The first epistle seems to have been well known by the early church fathers, who attributed it to the apostle John, the author of the Fourth Gospel. Clement of Alexandria, who mentions "the greater epistle," must also have known at least two of the three letters. Origen, who died in A.D. 253, mentions all three epistles.[1] Eusebius quoted Papias and inferred that there were two different Johns. "But Papias' statement is itself too ambiguous to provide much guidance, for he also appears to call the disciples themselves 'elders,' and Eusebius might therefore have been wrong to infer that Papias was actually referring to two different people called John."[2]

The external witness favors John the apostle as author of all the letters.

As one compares the Fourth Gospel with 1 John, and 1 John with the other two epistles, one notices close affinities. The language is similar, and they often use the same words and phrases:

- The fullness of joy (1 John 1:4; John 16:24)
- Keeping His commandments (1 John 2:3; John 14:15)
- The true light that shines/gives light (1 John 2:8; John 1:9)
- Abiding (1 John 2:24; John 15:4)
- Loving each other (1 John 3:11; John 15:12)
- The Spirit of truth (1 John 4:6; John 14:17)
- The Savior of the world (1 John 4:14; John 4:42)
- Being born of God (1 John 2:29; John 1:13)
- Having life (1 John 5:11; John 3:36)
- Life in Jesus (1 John 5:11, 12; John 1:4)

There are similarities in syntax and grammar, in structure, word order, themes, and pairing of opposites as well. However, one can also find differences. For instance, the "Advocate/Comforter" mentioned in 1 John 2:1 and in John 14:16 is primarily the Holy Spirit in the Gospel, but in 1 John, it is clearly Jesus. Though both the Fourth Gospel and 1 John begin with a reference to the Word, the Gospel of John stresses His *divinity* while 1 John focuses on eyewitnesses of His *humanity.* First John may have a stronger future hope than is presented in John's Gospel.

However, differences have to be expected due to the different objectives and audiences. The Fourth Gospel and the letters are complementary. It has been suggested that the statements on Jesus' divinity in the Gospel of John were misunderstood by people who tended toward gnostic teachings (an early heresy in the church). The apostle, then, wrote 1 John—which emphasizes that Christ was completely human and not just divine—to correct them.[3]

The references in 1 John to the apostles as eyewitnesses also provide an argument in favor of John the apostle as being the author of this epistle. The author of 1 John includes himself, stating "*We* have seen with our eyes . . ." (1 John 1:1; also 1:2, 3; 4:14). Furthermore, the author seems to be an elderly man—he addresses the church members as "my little children" (1 John 2:1) or "children" (1 John 2:12, 18; 3:18; 5:21) and calls himself "the elder" in 2 and 3 John.

Turning to the similarities between the letters, we notice that they share common vocabulary and ideas:

- Walking in the truth/light (2 John 4; 1 John 1:7)
- The new commandment (2 John 5; 1 John 2:8)
- Loving each other (2 John 5; 1 John 3:11)
- The existence of antichrists (2 John 7; 1 John 2:18, 22; 4:3)
- Truth (2 John 1; 3 John 1; 1 John 1:6)
- Love (2 John 3; 3 John 6; 1 John 2:5)

The evidence strongly favors John as the author of the epistles attributed to him.

The first letter may be addressed to the Christian communities in which John served and that knew him. The second letter is addressed "to the chosen Lady and her children" (2 John 1), either an individual[4] or a local church.[5] Third John is directly addressed to a specific person. The two shorter books may have fitted on a single papyrus sheet each. Thus, the availability (or lack of availability) of writing material may have been a factor in the length of the two documents.

The doctrines of the false teachers fit quite well into a situation toward the end of the first century, as does the problem with Diotrephes, who usurped power and opposed the apostle. That would place the letters after the Gospel of John. As to the date of writing, the early nineties of the first century can be assumed.[6]

II. What: The Content of the Epistles

1. First John

First John starts with an eyewitness account. "We have heard" occurs three times in 1 John 1:1–5, "we have seen" four times,[7] "we have touched" once, and "has appeared to us" also once. The apostolic proclamation is mentioned three times in these verses. What the apostles have experienced and proclaim is the "Word of life" and "what was from the beginning." Although some suggest that the "Word of life" is the apostolic tradition, it surely refers to Jesus. In this case, the prologues of John and 1 John would have in common the reference to Jesus as the Word. This fits very well the context of 1 John, in which Christology is a major problem. John's intention was that the apostolic proclamation of Jesus would lead to fellowship within the church and with the Father and the Son.

First John 1:6–10 deals with the issue of sin. Two positive verses containing the promise of forgiveness of sin are embedded between three negative verses. The topic of sin is continued in chapter 2. Then obedience and love are introduced (2:3–5). Again John provides a reason for writing his letter (2:12–14): he reminds his audience that they know or have known God and do not need to accept strange new teachings about Jesus. The warning not to love the world follows (2:15–17). The last part of chapter 2 deals with warnings about antichrists. In the beginning of chapter 3, John mentions Christians' privilege of being children of God and of being like God in a certain respect (3:1, 2). This privilege must lead us to avoid sin (3:3–10). The remaining part of John 3 discusses love (3:11–24), which cannot consist only of words but must lead to merciful action.

Chapter 4 returns to false teachers (4:1–6), followed by a passage dealing with love (4:7–21). The famous statement that God is love comes in this chapter (4:8). This love has become evident in the incarnation and sacrifice of Jesus Christ. God's love must lead us to love each other.

In 1 John 5, the topic "faith" is quite prominent. At the end of the passage we hear about eternal life, which is available only in the Son. A significant verse is 5:13, which talks about the assurance of salvation, followed in the next two verses by assurance that God hears and answers prayer. The remainder of chapter 5 returns to the issue of sin, the devil, and Jesus Christ.

It is difficult to determine the structure of 1 John. The author does not move forward in a linear way; related themes appear again and again. Therefore, it has been suggested that John presents his arguments in a cyclic way, revisiting his topics from different angles.[8]

Smalley suggests two main sections in 1 John:

Preface (1:1–4): The Word of Life
Live in the Light (1:5–2:29)

God is light (1:5–7)
First condition: renounce sin (1:8–2:2)
Second condition: be obedient (2:3–11)
Third condition: reject worldliness (2:12–17)
Fourth condition: keep the faith (2:18–29)

Live as Children of God (3:1–5:13)

God is Father (3:1–3)
First condition: renounce sin (3:4–9)
Second condition: be obedient (3:10–24)
Third condition: reject worldliness (4:1–6)
Fourth condition: be loving (4:7–5:4)
Fifth condition: keep the faith (5:5–13)

Conclusion (5:14–21): Christian Confidence[9]

Others opt for three major sections—for instance, "God Is Light" (1:5–2:27), "God Is Righteous" (2:28–4:6), and "God Is Love" (4:7–5:12).[10] Each suggestion seems to point to aspects that are useful and that increase our understanding of the epistle.

2. SECOND JOHN

In the second epistle, the apostle expresses his thankfulness that the lady's children walk in the truth. He also talks about love and obedience and focuses on the false teachers whom church members must avoid. In the conclusion, John expresses his wish to visit his audience and transmits greetings. Terian suggests the following outline for 2 John:

Introduction (1–3)
Message (4–11)

Praise for faithfulness (4)
Exhortation to continue in love (5–6)
Warning against false teachers (7–11)

Conclusion (12, 13)[11]

3. THIRD JOHN

The third letter is addressed to Gaius, who is commended for his faithfulness and encouraged not to give up and to continue to be hospitable in spite of problems with Diotrephes. Next, John talks about Diotrephes, who seems to rule the church with an iron fist and even opposes the apostle himself. After that he mentions Demetrius. As in 2 John, he expresses his hope to meet with the recipient of his letter, and he sends greetings. Terian outlines the letter in the following way:

Introduction (1)
Message (2–12)
  Good wishes and satisfaction (2–4)
  Hospitality praised (5–8)
  Hostility opposed (9, 10)
  A lesson and recommendation (11, 12)
Conclusion (13, 14)[12]

III. WHY: THE PURPOSE OF THESE LETTERS

1. FIRST JOHN

The first letter of John makes strong statements about false teachers, calling them antichrists. The term is found four times in 1 John and once in 2 John and nowhere else in the Bible, although the theological concept does appear in other places. These antichrists' erroneous ideas about Jesus needed rebuttal and correction, as did the practical implications of their teachings.

Repeatedly, John tells us about the purpose for writing this letter: "so that our joy may be complete" (1 John 1:4); "because your sins have been forgiven. . . . Because you know Him who is from the beginning. . . . Because you have conquered the evil one" (2:12–14); "so that you may know that you have eternal life" (5:13).

These statements are reaffirming; many focus on Jesus. However, read in their contexts, it becomes evident that there was a false sense of security, a false claim of knowledge, and some serious doctrinal problems in the churches that received these letters. In the midst of all this, the author portrays a positive picture of true Christianity and focuses on its positive nature. And he appeals to the faithful church members, encouraging them and letting them know that ethics and a proper understanding of Jesus Christ go together.

2. SECOND AND THIRD JOHN

The purpose of 2 John is to warn what probably was a house church against traveling teachers who espouse the erroneous teachings and ethics of the false teachers mentioned in 1 John. In both cases, they are called "antichrists."

In 3 John, a power struggle seems to be an issue. Diotrephes attempts to usurp all authority. John supports Gaius, a loyal church member who is still willing to care for traveling brothers, whereas Diotrephes disfellowships those who are hospitable. "We might . . . speculate that Diotrephes was using the danger of heresy to build his own power base."[13] While John encourages Gaius, he criticizes Diotrephes.

IV. Jesus in the Johannine Epistles

Jesus is found throughout John's epistles. Many names and descriptions characterize Him. He is (1) the Word of life (1 John 1:1), (2) the Life (1 John 1:2; 5:20), (3) the Son of the Father (1 John 1:3; 4:14; 2 John 3), (4) the Son (1 John 2:22–24; 2 John 9), (5) the Son of God (1 John 3:8; 4:15), (6) the Christ (1 John 1:3; 2:22; 5:1), (7) our Advocate (1 John 2:1), (8) the True Light (1 John 2:8), (9) the Savior (1 John 4:14), (10) the True God (1 John 5:20), and (11) the Truth (3 John 12).

Faithful church members, as well as false teachers, may have largely agreed on the nature of the Father, but they disagreed on Jesus' divinity. Therefore, the emphasis throughout the first two letters is on Jesus Christ. The issue was whether or not Jesus "has come in the flesh" (1 John 4:2) and "is the Christ" (2:22).

What we read about Christ's nature is that He is from the beginning (1:1). He is righteous (2:1, 29; 3:7) and pure (3:3). There is no sin in Him (3:5). He has come in the flesh (4:2) and is called the One born of God (5:18). This all points to His incarnation—that is, when the Divine Lord became a human being.

John clearly maintains that it is impossible to separate Father and Son. Even in our days, some people think they can have a relationship with God the Father without caring about Jesus. For them, Jesus is just a wonderful human being. John, however, is clear: if you know about Jesus but do not accept Him as Messiah and Son of God, you cannot have a relationship with God the Father. This does not mean that John proposes a kind of modalism, in which Father, Son, and Holy Spirit are appearances of the same Divine Person. While several times John doesn't clearly distinguish the Father and the Son (see 1 John 2:25, 29; 5:20), he may have intentionally been ambiguous in these cases to stress the unity he saw between Father and Son. Both Father and Son are God. First John contains 105 verses, and Jesus occurs in about 45 of them. This affirms that Jesus is at the center of 1 John.

V. JESUS' MINISTRY IN JOHN'S EPISTLES

Not only do the Johannine letters portray Jesus from different perspectives, but they also emphasize His ministry.

His incarnation brings about our salvation. First John clearly refers to Christ's incarnation (4:2, 9). It is not possible to separate the human Jesus from the so-called Divine Christ. Jesus Christ is one Person, completely human and yet divine. Jesus Christ has come in the flesh (1 John 4:2; 2 John 7)—that is, He became a human being like us and lived a human life as we do—not for His own sake but for ours. The preexistent Jesus was sent as the "only" Son in the world so that we may live (1 John 4:9). Christ came by water and blood (1 John 5:6). He came to destroy the works of the devil (1 John 3:8). Jesus differed from us in that, in contrast to all of us, in Him was and is no sin (1 John 3:5).

His death brings about our salvation. Both Jesus' life as a human being and His death on the cross were essential. His death is clearly salvific—1:7; 2:2; 3:5, 16; 4:9, 14. It is the cross of Jesus and the blood of Jesus that save us, nothing else. Today, when some Christians tell us that we can obtain forgiveness of sin without Jesus' substitutionary death, when they praise the Father for allegedly forgiving our shortcomings independent of the sacrifice of His Son, and when they even declare that Jesus' death on the cross was not a sacrifice but a call to awaken us to search for God, John reminds us, "The blood of Jesus His Son cleanses us from all sin" (1:7).

Jesus as our Advocate. However much we might hate sin and fight against it, we still may fall. In such a case, we have Jesus as an Advocate through whom atonement is brought (2:1, 2).

Jesus as the Giver of the Holy Spirit. In 1 John, the Holy Spirit is described with the term *anointing.* Believers have received the anointing from Jesus (2:27), who teaches us "all things."

Jesus' message and His commandments. Jesus' message is that God is light (1:5). He has given commandments, which His followers should keep (2:3; 4:21)—especially the commandments to love each other and to love God.

Jesus cares for those who believe in Him. Jesus, as the One born of God, keeps God's children safe; the devil cannot touch them (5:18). Jesus also offers mercy and peace to believers (2 John 3). He provides eternal life and wants us to have assurance (1 John 2:25; 5:11–13).

Jesus will come again. Finally, there is the promise that Jesus will come again (2:28; 3:2). The future coming of the Lord is not only a wonderful hope but also a strong incentive for His followers to live a holy and righteous life.

How are Jesus' followers to react to all that He has done for humankind? John answers: We are called to obey Jesus' commandments (2:3) and to have a correct knowledge of Him (2:4). We are challenged to keep His Word (2:5) and to walk as He did (2:6). We should remain in Him (2:27). Those who do right are born of Him (2:29), and one day we will be like Him (3:2). Therefore, we are to purify ourselves (3:3). We are called to believe in the name of the Son, Jesus Christ (3:23), and to abide in His teaching (2 John 9).

CONCLUSION

The Johannine epistles give us a glimpse of the church at the end of the first century. We have noticed two major problems: false teachings leading to a false lifestyle, and a leadership problem within the church. The false teachings may be called proto-gnosticism and would later grow into full-blown gnosticism. In order to exercise control, the leadership of the church would later assume more and more authority until the bishop would rule almost like a king and the papal system would evolve. The solution to the problems John sees instead is a correct understanding of Jesus—His nature, character, teachings, and ethics—and an intimate walk with Him.

CHAPTER 2

Experiencing the Word of Life (1 John 1:1–4)

Witnesses are important in courts. Their testimony can contribute to a person's being convicted or declared not guilty. They are also important in everyday life. They may have experienced healing through a specific cure. They may have received comfort and help from a Christian counselor, pastor, or friend and are willing not only to share their experience but also to recommend the person who helped them.

In the introduction to his first letter, John affirms that he belongs to the circle of eyewitnesses who have seen and experienced Jesus and are able to share life-transforming information with others. In a community in which some may have denied Jesus' divinity or His humanity and some thought that they could have fellowship with God the Father without Jesus, John's testimony is crucial.

In our days in which it is politically incorrect to claim that the biblical Jesus is the only way to salvation, this testimony must be heard again and afresh.

I. The Introduction to John's First Letter (1 John 1:1–4)

1. Summary

First John 1:1–4 forms the introduction to the first letter of John. First John 1:1–3 consists of one long sentence, which some translations have broken down into smaller units. John points out that he, together with others, is an eyewitness of the "Word of life." Verse 2 is an insertion explaining "life." Then a twofold statement follows: First, the acceptance of "life" leads to fellowship;

and second, its acceptance allows for complete joy. John wants his audience to experience joy and fellowship. This becomes possible if they accept Jesus and salvation through Him as proclaimed by the apostles.

2. STRUCTURE

Like other biblical authors, John uses repetition of words in verses 1–4 to drive home his point.

v. 1 1. What was from the beginning,
2. what WE HAVE HEARD,
3. *WHAT WE HAVE SEEN* with our eyes,
4. what we have looked at
5. and our hands have touched concerning the Word of **life**—

v. 2 (insertion)
and the life <u>was manifested</u>,
and *WE HAVE SEEN*
and we testify
and ***<u>we proclaim</u>*** to you the eternal **life,**
which was with the **<u>Father</u>**
and **<u>was manifested</u>** to us—

v. 3 6. what *WE HAVE SEEN*
7. and WE HAVE HEARD
<u>we proclaim</u> to you also,
<u>so that</u> you too may have FELLOWSHIP *with* us;
and indeed our FELLOWSHIP is *with* the ***<u>Father</u>,*** and *with* his Son Jesus Christ.

v. 4 These things we write,
<u>so that</u> our joy may be made complete.

This presentation allows us to see the dynamics of these verses. It begins with a long subordinate clause consisting of seven elements (see above). Elements 2 through 7 depend on the first ("what was from the beginning") and express how the eyewitnesses related to it. Elements 2 and 3, which refer to hearing and seeing, are repeated in reversed order as elements 6 and 7. They encompass and reinforce the experience of the eyewitnesses. The fifth element, "our hands have touched," is expanded by the phrase "concerning the Word of life."

The insertion (v. 2) develops the concept of "life." This insertion begins and ends with the verb "to manifest." As "hearing and seeing" encircle the experience of the eyewitnesses, so "being manifested" brackets verse 2's exposition of the revelation of life personified in the person of Jesus Christ. Not only does this insertion explain the last word of verse 1, it also prepares for the main clause in verse 3b that follows the long list of "whats." How does it do that? By introducing the concept of proclaiming what was seen and by mentioning the heavenly Father.

While verses 1 and 2 focus on the "life" that the eyewitnesses experienced, verse 3 focuses on the "fellowship" that has become possible through the proclamation of "life." This fellowship has two dimensions: fellowship with the eyewitnesses and fellowship with the Father and the Son.

The long sentence ends in verse 3: "This we proclaim to you so that you may have fellowship." Whatever John and the apostles have experienced must be proclaimed. The "Word of life" must be shared. John wants his hearers and readers to have a genuine relationship with God and to know and remain in the True Jesus, not the one manufactured by those who have not met Him but are involved in heresy. The stakes are high because they involve the gain or loss of eternal life.

3. THE FUNCTION OF 1 JOHN 1:1–4

The first letter of John differs from other letters because its prologue replaces the usual formal greetings and mention of the author and audience. Through this prologue, John establishes his authority, connects to his audience, and provides a preview of what is to come. It contains at least some of the basic concerns of the letter, as well as important vocabulary that will be used again later:

- The eyewitnesses have seen, heard, and touched *Jesus.* They call Him Jesus Christ, indicating that the human Jesus cannot be separated from the Divine Christ (1 John 1:1–3). Jesus is indeed the Christ, the Messiah (2:22; 5:1).
- Jesus is the *Son* of God. The term *Son,* which first appears in 1 John 1:3, occurs another twenty-one times in 1 John. It always refers to Jesus and in all cases is related to God the Father. John shows that people cannot have fellowship with God without having fellowship with Jesus.
- In the prologue, God is twice introduced as the *Father* (1:2, 3). The

name "God" occurs only from verse 5 onward. In 1 John, the term *Father*—used twelve times in the singular—refers always to God. He is presented as Father, and believers are His "children" (3:1), indicating intimate relationship and pointing forward to the topic *love* that John will develop.

- The prologue mentions *life* three times (1:1, 2, 2). "Eternal life" occurs in 1:2; 2:25; 3:15; 5:11, 13, 20. In 5:20, Jesus is identified with eternal life in such a way that the text comes closest to 1 John 1:2. First John begins with Jesus Christ as eternal life and concludes with Him as God and eternal life. Eternal life is not just a new quality of life that is offered to those who believe in the Son, it has to do with and refers to the Son Himself.
- The concept of *fellowship* is stressed in 1 John 1:3, 3, 6, 7, and later to some extent through the frequent use of the term *remaining/abiding.*
- The *manifestation* of the life (1:2, 2) is the appearance of Jesus. It refers not only to the first coming of Jesus, His incarnation, as in 1 John 1:2, 2; 3:5, 8; 4:9, but also describes His future second coming (2:28; 3:2).
- The eyewitnesses *"testify"* and *"proclaim"* eternal life (1:2, 3, NIV). This activity is not limited to human beings (4:14), but the Holy Spirit (5:6, 7) and God the Father also testify (5:9, 10).

These are some connections between the prologue and the rest of the letter. Indeed, the prologue sets the tone for the rest of the epistle.

II. First John 1 and John 1

It is intriguing that the prologue of the first letter of John reminds the reader of the prologue of the Gospel of John (John 1:1–18). Although there are differences between the passages, there are also a number of similarities.

1. Similarities

- The passages begin almost identically. Both talk about the beginning (John 1:1; 1 John 1:1).
- Both prologues introduce important themes and issues and contain vocabulary that will be found throughout the body of each document.
- Both mention the incarnated *Word* (John 1:1; 1 John 1:1), which points to Jesus Christ (John 1:14, 17; 1 John 1:3).
- Both refer to the issue of *life* (John 1:4; 1 John 1:1, 2).

- One says that the Word was with God (John 1:1), and the other that the eternal life was with the Father (1 John 1:2). However, God as a Father is also found in John 1:14.
- The very same verbal form translated "we have seen" is found in John 1:14 and 1 John 1:1.
- *Testimony* is an important concept in the Johannine literature. Both the verb form and the noun form are found frequently in the Gospel of John, 1 John, 3 John, and Revelation. The testimony of eyewitnesses is not restricted to 1 John but is also found in the Gospel; for example, John 1:34; 21:24.
- The concept of light appears in John 1:4, 5, 7–9 and also in 1 John 1:5, which is the verse directly following the prologue.

2. DIFFERENCES

Differences between the two prologues are mainly a matter of emphasis.

- The prologue to the Gospel of John (1:1–18) is much longer than the concise prologue of 1 John.
- The Gospel emphasizes Jesus' role as God and Creator. He created everything; no created being came into existence without Him. This is not found in the prologue of 1 John.
- In the introduction to 1 John, Jesus is not directly called God as He is in the prologue to John. In fact, 1 John may more strongly emphasize His humanity.
- In 1 John, the apostle emphasizes the role of eyewitnesses and their proclamation more than he does in the prologue to his Gospel.
- Although the introduction to John's Gospel speaks of God as Father, this concept does not dominate the introduction as it does the prologue of 1 John.
- The verb "to believe" is introduced in John 1:7, 12 and is used almost a hundred times throughout the Gospel. It is also found in 1 John but only from chapter 3 onward.

3. THE PROLOGUE OF THE GOSPEL OF JOHN AND THE TEXT OF 1 JOHN

Table 1 shows some of the unique and crucial concepts found in both John's Gospel and his first letter. The table does not contain the parallels already noted in the two prologues. This table may indicate that the Gospel of John forms the background to John's epistles. An understanding of the Gospel may help one better understand 1 John.

TABLE 1. COMPARISON OF KEY CONCEPTS IN THE GOSPEL OF JOHN AND 1 JOHN

Terms/Phrases	*Gospel of John*	*First Letter of John*
Light	1:4, 5, 7–9; 3:19–21; etc.	1:5, 7; 2:8–10
The light shines	1:5	2:8
The True Light	1:9	2:8
Darkness	1:5; 8:12; etc.	1:5; 2:8, 9, 11
Witness	1:7; 3:11, 32, 33; etc.	5:9–11
To believe	1:7, 12, 50; 2:11, 22; etc.	3:23; 4:1, 16; 5:1, 5, 10, 13
True	1:9; 7:28; 8:16; etc.	2:8; 5:20
World	1:9, 10, 29; 3:16, 17, 19; etc.	2:2, 15–17; 3:1, 13, 17; etc.
To know	1:10, 48; 6:69; 7:17; etc.	2:3–5, 13, 14, 18, 29; etc.
To receive	1:12, 16; 3:11, 27, 32, 33; etc.	2:27; 3:22; 5:9
To give	1:12, 17, 22; 3:16, 27, 34; etc.	3:1, 23, 24; 4:13; 5:11, 16, 20
Children of God	1:12; 11:52	3:1, 2, 10; 5:2
His name	1:12; 2:23; 20:31	2:12
The name of the Son	3:18	3:23; 5:13
Born of God	1:13	3:9; 4:7; 5:1, 4, 18
Blood	1:13; 6:53–56; 19:34; etc.	1:7; 5:6, 8
Flesh	1:13, 14; 3:6; 6:51–56; etc.	2:16; 4:2
Will	1:13; 4:34; 5:30; 6:38; etc.	2:17; 5:14
The only begotten	1:14, 18; 3:16, 18	4:9
Truth	1:14, 17; 3:21; 4:23, 24; etc.	1:6, 8; 2:4, 21; 3:18, 19; etc.
To say	1:15, 22; 8:13, 33, 39; etc.	1:6, 8, 10; 2:4, 6, 9; etc.
To see	1:18, 34; 4:45; 6:36; etc.	1:1–3; 3:6; 4:20; etc.

III. THE WORD OF LIFE (1 JOHN 1:1, 2)

The introduction to 1 John deals with the "Word (*logos*) of life" that was seen, heard, touched, and proclaimed by the eyewitnesses. John 1:1–3 says the "Word" was with God and was God, and all things were created through the Word. According to John 1:14, the Word became a human being and is the Son of God. He is Jesus Christ.

In Revelation 19, a rider on a white horse appears followed by the army of heaven. He is called "Faithful and True," and He judges with justice (Rev. 19:11). He is the King of kings and Lord of lords crowned with many crowns

(Rev. 19:12–16). The fact that the title "King of kings and Lord of Lords" belongs to the Lamb indicates that this Person is Jesus (Rev. 17:14), who died to purchase humans with His blood (Rev. 5:9). This majestic Being is also called "the Word of God" (Rev. 19:13). Since in the other Johannine literature the term *word* may in certain contexts refer to a person and designate Jesus, it is conceivable that in 1 John 1:1 it also stands for Jesus.

The same is true for the term *life*. In John 14:6, Jesus called Himself "the Way, and the Truth, and the Life." The Life in 1 John 1:2 also refers to Jesus. However, since John says, "*What* was from the beginning, *what* we have heard, *what* we have seen" (using a neuter pronoun), instead of "*Who* was from the beginning, *whom* we have heard and seen" (employing a masculine pronoun), the reference could be to the good news of the gospel of Christ rather than to Jesus. However, this is unlikely. Expositors suggest that the reference is to Jesus in spite of the grammar or to both Jesus and the message about Him.[1] Raymond Brown proposes that the neuter pronouns "cover the person, the words, and the works" of Jesus.[2]

Why should we connect *the Word* with Jesus? (1) The eyes and hands in verse 1 must be understood literally. Although it is possible to hear the gospel of Jesus with one's ears, it is more difficult to see it with the eyes, but it is practically impossible to touch it with one's hands. Hearing, seeing, and touching a person makes more sense than hearing, seeing, and touching the gospel. (2) Being "with the Father" (1:2) favors a person rather than a message. And in verse 2, the Life and the Father are linked, and the following verse puts Christ in the same position. (3) "*Him* who was from the beginning" (2:13, 14) points to a person. Because the same phrase "from the beginning" is used here and in the prologue, it seems likely that it refers to Jesus in both places. (4) The clause "the Life . . . was with the Father and has appeared to us" (1:2) also suggests that John had a person in mind. The word *to appear/to be manifested* is used in 1 John 2:28; 3:2, 5, 8 to point to Jesus' first and second comings. Thus, the passage should be understood in the following way:

Jesus is the Word of life that was from the beginning, the Eternal Life that was seen, heard, and touched. He is divine. Through Him, God speaks to us. The human Jesus and the Divine Christ are the same Person. "In short," writes Akin, "John's central purpose is to encourage his readers to persevere in their belief in the apostolic proclamation of the Christ as Jesus, the incarnate Son of God."[3]

Life always depends on Jesus; apart from Him, there is no life and also no immortal soul. However, since Jesus is life eternal, that life is also granted to those who believe in Him (5:11–13). Witherington notes, "Eternal life . . . refers not just to life everlasting, though that is meant as well, but furthermore to a different quality of life, an unending spiritual life that has unlimited potential. . . . It is a life that binds the believer forever to God and to other believers. As such, it already transcends time, for we have it already in time, but it will go beyond the temporal existence that we now experience."[4]

Why should Christians be concerned to have a correct understanding of Jesus? Because to know and to have Jesus means to have this new and wonderful life.

IV. EYEWITNESSES (1 JOHN 1–3)

In the prologue to John's first epistle, a change from "we" to "you" and back to "we" takes place. The "we" in verses 1 and 2 refers to the eyewitnesses. Among them is the author of 1 John. The "you" is his audience, people who were not eyewitnesses of Christ's life here on earth. But what about verse 4? Some manuscripts read "your joy" while others favor "our joy." Generally, scholars favor "our joy."[5] While the eyewitnesses and the audience are separated in verses 1–3, in verse 4, both groups are united in common joy.

Eyewitnesses are people who have observed a historical event, for instance, a sports event or a concert, an accident, or a crime, and who, if not severely handicapped, are able to share what they have experienced. Scripture frequently uses the concept of eyewitnesses. Joshua was an eyewitness of what the Lord had done during the Exodus (Deut. 3:21; Josh. 24:7). After the queen of Sheba had met with Solomon, she confessed that what she had heard was only half of what she had seen (1 Kings 10:7; 2 Chron. 9:6). Isaiah saw God on His throne and became an eyewitness of the heavenly world (Isa. 6:5). According to 1 Corinthians 15:3–8, a vast group of eyewitnesses—including the apostles—confirmed the death and resurrection of Christ. Stott states, "To have *heard* was not enough; people 'heard' God's voice in the Old Testament. To have *seen* was more compelling. But to have *touched* was the conclusive proof of material reality, that the Word 'became flesh, and lived for a while among us.' "[6]

Today we cannot be direct eyewitnesses of the Christ event. This is not possible. Jesus no longer lives among us. But we still can believe in Him (John 20:29) by relying on the eyewitness accounts in Scripture and experiencing Him in our daily walk. Indirectly, we still can see Him, hear Him, and touch Him.

The Bible confirms that we can see God/Jesus indirectly, though not physically. Although Job had not directly seen God, he confessed, "I had heard of you by the hearing of the ear, but now my eye sees you" (Job 42:5). Simeon, holding the Child Jesus in his arms, exclaimed, "My eyes have seen your salvation" (Luke 2:30). He physically saw the Child, but it was not directly evident that this Child would bring salvation. In Revelation 17:6, the witnesses of Jesus are not the eyewitnesses of the first-century church. Christians throughout the centuries are called to become witnesses for what God had done in history and in their lives.

According to Acts 19:13–16, Jewish exorcists who had a superficial knowledge of Jesus tried to use His name in a magical way in an exorcism rite—without success. It is not sufficient to invoke "the Jesus whom Paul preached." We must preach the biblical Jesus, and in order for our witness to have integrity and persuasion, we must know the Lord ourselves. Such a witness can be very attractive and powerful, especially in a postmodern world.

V. FELLOWSHIP OF THE SAINTS (1 JOHN 1:3, 4)

The last part of the prologue deals with the purpose of the proclamation of the Word of life. John mentions two reasons: fellowship and joy. Stott talks about "the divine order—*angelia, koinōnia, chara*"[7]—that is, "proclamation, fellowship, joy."

John invites his audience and even us today to accept his testimony about Jesus and thereby experience fellowship. The proclamation of Jesus builds community and affects future generations. To accept Jesus as Savior and Lord, as Giver of eternal life, means to be added to the family of believers and to enjoy fellowship with God and Jesus.

Jesus had established His community or church (Matt. 16:18; John 10:14–16). The proclamation of Jesus brings people into fellowship with the Father and the Son and also into fellowship with His church. There is not only an unseen heavenly connection but also a very real, visible connection to other believers. Witherington states, "The two sorts of fellowship are intertwined and interdependent, and the Son is the source of both kinds of fellowship."[8] And Stott explains, "Our fellowship with each other arises from, and depends on our fellowship with God."[9] Christians are blessed by the fact that they do not have to master their lives alone but have become part of Christ's family. Fellowship also includes the concept of mutual sharing and partnership. "Christian fellowship is not the sentimental and superficial attachment of a random collection of individuals, but the profoundly mutual relationship of those who remain 'in Christ,' and therefore belong to each other."[10]

This understanding of fellowship militates against the individualism of our days, which wants to be united to Jesus in baptism yet have nothing to do with His church. It also militates against a concept of fellowship that is based on "a superficial social camaraderie instead of a spiritual fellowship with the Father and his Son Jesus Christ."[11]

The prologue ends with verse 4. John's second goal is to have the believers' joy completed. Verse 4 looks certainly back to the preceding verses—our joy is completed because Jesus, life eternal, has appeared and fellowship with God and the community of believers has become possible. It may also look forward to the rest of 1 John, in which Jesus and salvation through Him as well as a life with God is unfolded. The joy of verse 4 may also envision the future appearance of our Lord. Thus, 1 John 1:1–4 may encompass the time from the preexistent Christ to the final consummation at Christ's second coming.

CONCLUSION

John's prologue not only challenges us to accept the testimony of the eyewitnesses and to experience the joy of fellowship with the Godhead and His church but also calls us to become witnesses ourselves. Knowing the eternal Word of life, Jesus, is a matter of life and death.

CHAPTER 3

Turning Away From Sin (1 John 1:5–2:2)

High in the Rocky Mountains a ranger nearly froze to death—until his dog, a Saint Bernard, managed to rouse the near-comatose man. "If that dog hadn't been with me, I'd be dead today," John Elliott says. "When you're freezing to death, you actually feel warm all over and don't wake up because it feels too good." Sin is also deceitful, and there is no chance of avoiding the harm it does (Rom. 6:23). We need help outside of ourselves.

In the second section of his first letter, John contrasts the character of God with the nature and behavior of humanity. While God is light, humans are involved in sin—which is so grievous that only God can bring about a solution. To live in sin means to live in darkness. To live in the light means to acknowledge and confess one's sin, renounce it, accept and use the divine provisions spelled out in 1 John 1; 2, and stop relying on ourselves to solve the sin problem.

I. The Character of God (1 John 1:5)

The prologue of 1 John (1:1–4) ends with an emphasis on fellowship and joy. How can we have fellowship with God? First, we have to know the character of God. Second, we have to live in such a way that our walk reflects the nature of God.

First John 1:5 introduces the fundamental statement of our passage. It portrays the character of God by pointing out that God is light. What follows depends on this declaration. "The next two sections of 1 John are on the theme of walking in the light. The first section, 1 John 1:5–2:2, addresses the theme in relation to the issue of sin, while the second section, 1 John 2:3–11, focuses on walking in the light in relation to obedience, especially to the love command."[1]

John declares that he heard from Jesus that God is light. The Gospels do not record such a statement from Jesus. But since the Gospels do not contain all of Jesus' sayings (John 20:30), He may have said it without it being recorded. More likely, John may not have been referring to a specific saying of Jesus. Repeatedly Jesus called Himself the Light (Matt. 4:16; John 3:19; 8:12; 12:46). He says He came to reveal the Father (John 1:18). Therefore, His nature and character are also the Father's nature and character. In Scripture, God is called Light or associated with light a number of times; see, for example, Psalms 27:1; 36:9; Isaiah 60:19, 20; 1 Timothy 6:16.

Stott notes, "Of the statements about the essential being of God, none is more comprehensive than *God is light.* It is his nature to reveal himself, as it is the property of the light to shine; and the revelation is of perfect purity and unutterable majesty."[2] One may distinguish several aspects of the image of light as attributed to God. First, light represents God's absolute truthfulness and integrity, His desire to reveal Himself, and His authenticity. God's revelation in Scripture is described in terms of light (Pss. 36:9; 119:105, 130). This facet could be called the intellectual aspect.

Second, the declaration that God is light speaks of a moral quality of His being—that He is absolutely righteous, good, holy, and pure.

Third, the physical dimension of light points to God's absolute glory and majesty and may even describe His transcendence, because in His light, God is unapproachable (1 Tim. 6:16). Yet, in Jesus, He has become the Light that we can see, hear, touch, and therefore experience.

Fourth, light is associated with life (John 1:4). The Father and Jesus as the Light are the Source of life. This may be understood as the existential aspect. It points to Him as the One who brings about salvation (Ps. 27:1).

The last part of 1 John 1:5 forms a contrast to the previous statement: "and darkness is not in Him at all." The double negative in Greek points to God's complete separation from sin and evil, error and ignorance. The apostle underlines in the strongest possible terms God's perfection and His distance from and opposition to sin. He is not comparable to the Greek or Roman gods, in whom one would find vices as well as virtues.

The mention of darkness introduces the following verses. As fallen beings, humans belong by nature to the sphere of darkness. However, they can become "children of light" (Eph. 5:8) and even "the light of the world" (Matt. 5:14). If that happens, they reflect their heavenly Father, though not perfectly. As long as they live on earth, they are involved in a struggle with darkness and their innate attraction to sin, and they must continuously remain committed to God.

II. THE SIN PROBLEM (1 JOHN 1:6, 8, 10)

1. AN OUTLINE OF 1 JOHN 1:6–10

Verses 6 through 10 of 1 John 1 form a well-structured unit. After his principal statement about God's character, John moves on to the attitudes and behavioral patterns of believers that are in contrast to the Divine Light. The focus of this section is on behavior—most of the verbs appear in the present tense, indicating ongoing patterns—rather than on theology, although the behavior is related to theological deliberations.

In the original Greek, all five verses begin with the term *if.* However, we notice a marked difference when we read on. Verses 6, 8, and 10 begin with the phrase "If we say/claim that . . ." All three of these verses are negative and do not reflect truth. The positions they record may have been taken by some of the believers whom John addresses. The "we" in 1 John 1:6–10 includes all Christians.[3]

Verses 7 and 9 are positive statements containing divine promises. The passage reminds us that oftentimes it is not very important what we claim. We may be completely mistaken. What counts is our acceptance of the divine promises of verses 7 and 9.

v. 6	If we say/claim . . .	—	negative
v. 7	If we walk . . .	—	*positive*
v. 8	If we say/claim . . .	—	negative
v. 9	If we confess . . .	—	*positive*
v. 10	If we say/claim . . .	—	negative

First John 1:6–2:2 deals with sin. Every verse refers to sin or sinning. The term *unrighteousness* in verse 9 may be a synonym for *sin.* John makes such a strong emphasis on sin right at the beginning of the body of his first letter because the sin problem affects God and humanity, and a correct understanding of the nature and effects of sin will influence our lifestyle and theology.

Those verses containing negative attitudes or self-evaluations and destructive behavior of believers are associated with each other.

Verse 6	***Verse 8***	***Verse 10***
If we say that	If we say that	If we say that
Darkness	Sin	Sinning
We lie	—	We make God a liar
No truth	no truth	—
—	(The truth) is not in us	(His Word) is not in us

2. THE CONTENT OF VERSES 6, 8, AND 10

Looking at verses 6, 8, and 10, one has the impression that a twofold intensification is taking place. On one hand, the claims become worse and worse: (1) walking in the darkness while claiming to have fellowship with God (v. 6); (2) claiming to have reached a sinless state (v. 8); and (3) claiming to have never sinned (v. 10). On the other hand, the evaluation of the believers' strange attitude and behavior becomes more and more serious: (1) "we lie and do not practice the truth" (v. 6); (2) "we are deceiving ourselves and the truth is not in us" (v. 8); and (3) "we make Him [God] a liar and His Word is not in us" (v. 10).

Verse 6. John includes himself among those who run the danger of claiming to live with God while walking in darkness. Witherington states, "What troubles our author is the inconsistency between one's faith talk and one's faith walk. . . . For our author there is no hard-and-fast line between belief and behavior, between theology and ethics. . . . Behavior matters just as belief does, and aberrations in either sphere can sever one from fellowship with the community and with God."[4]

Verse 7, which gives the positive answers to the negative behavior in verse 6, helps to clarify the text. Instead of walking in darkness, one should walk in the light. What is darkness according to 1 John? It is hating one's brother (2:9–11). It is also contrasted with being cleansed from sin (1:7); therefore, to walk in darkness has to do with living in sin. Akin believes the text refers to those who reject Jesus as God's incarnate Son.[5] But this is disputed, because—so Witherington says—the false teachers are no longer part of the community (2:19) and are not included in the "we."[6] Within the Johannine community are believers who disregard or hate their Christian brothers and sisters and live an immoral life. John informs them that in reality they live in darkness. He challenges them to live in the light, which will lead to fellowship with believers. The surprising shift from fellowship with God (v. 6) to fellowship with each other (v. 7) shows where part of the problem lies. One cannot have fellowship with God without having fellowship with His children. One cannot have fellowship with God and continue to live in sin.

Verse 8. In verse 6, the issue is that people live a sinful life and either deny it or hold that sin does not matter. Verse 8 goes a step further. People do not necessarily deny that they have committed sin in the past, but they are convinced that they have attained a sinless condition. This may be the same group that was mentioned in verse 6.

The term *sin* is found seventeen times in 1 John—eleven times in the singular and six times in the plural. Here, sin is used in the singular, as it is in verse 7. It may refer to the basic sin of living our lives independent of God. However, in verses 9 and 10, the issue is sinful acts rather than sin as a condition. But the author does not always differentiate sharply between a sinful disposition and sinful acts[7] because in some cases—such as the "all sin" in verse 7 that points to each and every sin—the singular includes the notion of individual acts of sin.

Verse 8 points out that people have fallen prey to self-deception. They no longer realize their need to be purified by the blood of Jesus (v. 7). Therefore, it is conceivable that they do not hold Jesus in high esteem. "He who deliberately rejects right and accepts an untruth, especially an untruth that makes him feel superior to others and independent of the Saviour, can never be sure that he will ever again be willing or able to discern the difference between right and wrong."[8]

Verse 10. As serious as it is to claim that one has reached sinlessness (v. 8), it is even more serious to claim "we have not sinned" at all (v. 10), no matter how sin is defined, whether as a condition or as an act. Such people deny the biblical testimony that all—except Jesus—are sinners. If the previous group believed themselves to have attained a status that makes them independent of Jesus, these people think they have no need of Jesus and His substitutionary death at all. "This is the most blatant of the three denials," writes Stott. "The heretics maintained that their superior enlightenment rendered them incapable of sinning."[9] Johnson suggests that these people were "gnostically inclined." They were offended by the death of Jesus and also by the idea that Christ had to become completely human. "Their own 'perfectionism' and high, yet self-deceived, spirituality could do without the cross, as modern psychologies of self-actualization and 'success' often do."[10]

The result is that these persons make God a liar, which is much worse than lying or deceiving oneself. If God cannot be trusted regarding the problem of sin, how can He be trusted at all?

III. POSITIVE RESPONSES TO THE SIN PROBLEM (1 JOHN 1:7, 9; 2:2)

The term *sin* does not occur in 2 John and 3 John, but we find it seventeen times in the Gospel of John and three times in the Apocalypse. We find definitions of sin in 1 John 3:4, where the apostle equates it with lawlessness, and in 1 John 1:9 and 5:17, where he calls it unrighteousness, which is opposed to the righteous God. In Revelation 18:5, sin stands parallel to "iniquity." It is departure from the will of God as revealed to us in Scripture—especially in the commandments. Sin is also opposed to truth. It alienates the person who commits it from God and leads to spiritual death. But the wonderful news is that in Christ, sin can be forgiven.

Verse 7. This verse stresses that if we walk in the divine light continuously, fellowship with the church of Christ will be established and the blood of Jesus will cleanse us from all sin. Both verbs "to have" and "to cleanse" are used in the present tense, pointing to ongoing activity.

The "blood of Jesus" points to Jesus' sacrificial death on the cross, which is "the effective antidote for sin in the believer's life,"[11] cleansing us from all sin. This is a divine promise regarding the solution of the sin problem. John is not talking here about a person coming to Christ for the first time and receiving forgiveness of sin. Rather, he has in mind Christian believers who need cleansing throughout their life. And, paradoxically, the closer these believers draw to God, the more they will feel the need of cleansing. This cleansing, therefore, may refer to the process of sanctification.[12] Stott suggests that it is more than forgiveness. Jesus "erases the stain of sin."[13]

The reference to "all sin" is crucial. No sin is so grievous, so big, that it cannot be forgiven. In the Old Testament, certain highhanded sins could not be atoned for by a sacrifice (Ps. 51:16; Exod. 21:12–14), "but in the case of the atoning death of Jesus, all sins and all kinds of sins have been atoned for."[14] The solution to the sin problem is found in Jesus and what He has done for us.

Verse 9. We need to be honest about ourselves. In order to allow for fellowship with God, we must confess our sins and accept the divine provisions. The text assumes that all humans are in need of forgiveness. At the same time, the verse reveals the character of God. By His nature, God is faithful and just and not capricious. He is faithful to His nature and to His covenant promises, which include forgiveness when people break the covenant and repent. What about His justice? "He is *faithful* to forgive because he has promised to do so, and *just* because his Son died for our sins."[15]

The term *to confess* in 1 John 1:9 can also mean "to admit," "to acknowledge." To whom should sins be confessed? The verse implies to God, because according to the next part of the verse, God is the One who forgives our sins. Confession of sins may also include public confession to those who were hurt through our sins. In the Johannine literature, the phrase *to confess* has a public aspect (see, for example, John 1:20; 1 John 2:23; Rev. 3:5). If we truly confess our sins—not just in a general way, but individually as we become aware of them—God forgives and purifies.

First John 1:9 has the force of a command. We should lay our sins before God. Then He will forgive us and purify us. Sin makes us guilty. We need *forgiveness.* Sin makes us unclean. We need *purification.* Although the terms could be used synonymously, it is also possible that *purification* goes further and implies the removal of the power of sin from the life of believers.

IV. THE CHRISTIANS' GOAL (1 JOHN 2:1)

John tries to keep his community from falling into extremes. One extreme is the denial of the problem of sin and the claim to have complete freedom from sin. The other extreme involves those who admit that even Christians are still affected by sin, have a nature with inclinations to sin, and here and there commit sinful acts. They may begin to take sinning lightly and find excuses for their sins.[16]

But believers can never take sin lightly. It cost Jesus' life, and despite His sacrifice, will cost humans their potential eternal life if they continue to sin habitually. So John balances his previous statements about sin with the call not to sin (1 John 2:1). "The Christian ideal remains not to sin."[17]

The context of John's call in 1 John 2:1 is still the issue of walking in the light, and according to this verse, to walk in the light means to renounce sin. John addresses his church members in a caring and intimate way, calling them "little children," and he tells them one reason he has written this letter: to tell them they must renounce sin completely.

Then, again, John balances his admonition not to sin with the other side of the coin: "but if we sin." The Greek aorist in this line implies that Christians may occasionally commit acts of sins without, however, habitually sinning. The goal of a disciple of Christ remains not to sin. Sincere Christians admit that they are sinners, confess their sins, and seek to live without sin. Unfortunately, sinning is always a possibility for church members. Therefore, they need Someone to help them resist temptation, but they also need Someone who intervenes for them when they have sinned. Christians cannot trust themselves and their inherent powers. They must always rely on Jesus.

V. THE CHRISTIANS' COMFORT (1 JOHN 2:1, 2)

First John 2:1, 2 contains wonderful statements that comfort repentant sinners and fill them with hope and courage. It is Jesus who secures forgiveness for us. How?

First, He is our Advocate who intervenes in our behalf. The Greek term *paraklētos* is found only in the Johannine literature. In John 14:16, 26; 15:26; 16:7, it is applied to the Holy Spirit, although Jesus indirectly refers to Himself as an Advocate too, when He calls the Holy Spirit "another Advocate" (John 14:16). In 1 John 2:1, the term is used for Jesus. *Paraklētos* has been translated various ways, for example, *comforter, helper, advocate, mediator,* or *intercessor.* It is a person called to the side of someone else and who stands up for that person. A *paraklētos* can be a person who helps a friend. John describes Jesus as an Advocate, and the author of the letter to the Hebrews designates Him as High Priest. The concept of atonement and intercession is present in both contexts (compare Heb. 7:25).[18]

Second, this Advocate is Jesus Christ, the Righteous One. Righteousness is attributed to God the Father in 1 John 1:9 and to the Son in 1 John 2:1. Jesus is God, and although He encountered sin, it did not contaminate Him. Because of His righteous character, He can intercede for us.

Third, our forgiveness is secured because through His sacrificial death, Jesus brought about *hilasmos.*[19] In the New Testament, this term is found only in 1 John 2:2 and 4:10. It occurs five times in the Old Testament, with various but related meanings. In Leviticus 25:9, it qualifies the word *day,* thereby referring to the Day of Atonement. In Numbers 5:8, it describes the ram sacrificed to bring atonement, and in Ezekiel 44:27, it refers to the sin offering.

In 1 John 2:2, *hilasmos* is translated "propitiation" by the King James Version (KJV), the New American Standard Bible, (NASB), and the English Standard Version (ESV), to name some translations. The Revised Standard Version

(RSV) rendered the term "expiation." The New Revised Standard Version (NRSV) and the New International Version (NIV) translate *hilasmos* as "atoning sacrifice."

What is the difference between these terms? *Propitiation* normally has to do with appeasing an angry God. "Expiation, by contrast, is not something of which God is the recipient . . . referring to the divine act of removing the defilement of or cleansing someone from sin, or covering or protecting someone from the consequences of sin."[20] This term sounds better today, because the biblical God is not associated with capricious pagan deities. However, by choosing the term *expiation* instead of *propitiation,* translators may be downplaying the concept of divine wrath referred to frequently in Scripture.

A number of scholars favor *propitiation* because the preposition *for/on behalf of* used in 1 John 2:2 seems to favor the term. In this case, however, *propitiation* should not be understood in terms of the pagan background that occurs in nonbiblical literature.[21] Stott states, "The Christian propitiation is quite different, not only in the character of the divine anger but in the means by which it is propitiated. It is an appeasement of the wrath of God by the love of God through the gift of God. The initiative is not taken by us, nor even by Christ, but by God himself in sheer unmerited love. His wrath is averted not by any external gift, but by his own self-giving to die the death of sinners."[22] The term *hilasmos* seems to include both propitiation and expiation, which may be reflected in the translation "atoning sacrifice" or "atonement."[23]

In this verse, John takes a stand against the false concept of sin and possibly also against the false understanding of Jesus promoted by his opponents. He portrays Jesus as the Christ who is Sacrifice and Intercessor. This implies that He lived a sinless life among us, died on the cross, rose from the dead, and ascended to heaven, where He intercedes for us.

The widening of salvation at the end of 1 John 2:2 to include a solution to the sin problem of the world and not just of the church is not a universalism that holds that all sins are automatically forgiven because of Christ's sacrifice. The context does not allow for such a position, and such a conclusion would require that John contradict himself. Salvation has been made available to everyone through Christ's atoning sacrifice, but it is up to us to decide if we want to live in sin or accept divine forgiveness.

CONCLUSION

Regarding this passage Ellen G. White wrote,

> None of the apostles and prophets ever claimed to be without sin. Men who have lived the nearest to God, men who would sacrifice life itself rather than knowingly commit a wrong act, men whom God has honored with divine light and power, have confessed the sinfulness of their nature. They . . . have trusted wholly in the righteousness of Christ. So will it be with all who behold Christ. . . .
>
> . . . The nearer we come to Jesus, and the more clearly we discern the purity of His character, the more clearly shall we see the exceeding sinfulness of sin, and the less shall we feel like exalting ourselves.

On the other hand, she also said, "The directions laid down in the word of God leave no room for compromise with evil."[24]

We must avoid the extremes on both sides and rely on Jesus for our salvation. However, when we talk about Him as our Advocate and take great comfort in the fact that He has provided forgiveness for our sins, we must not give the impression that the Father is a stern person who must be persuaded by a go-between to forgive us. It was the Father who in His great love sent His only Son and secured our salvation.

CHAPTER 4

Keeping His Commandments (1 John 2:3–11)

While people proudly call themselves law-abiding citizens, these same people may not appreciate the idea of obedience to God's commandments. To some persons, obedience means unacceptable submission and loss of personal freedom. They consider God's law a terrible thing, something opposed to His grace and love.

At the beginning of the next section of his first letter, John emphasizes that to know God means to keep His commandments. However, prevalent customs and worldviews affect even Christian families. Biblical commands, for instance, concerning sexuality, health, and occult activities are being abandoned in favor of society and culture.

This problem is not new. According to Matthew 15:3–9 and Mark 7:6–13, Judaism of the first century, by the *corban* provision, set aside the commandment to honor father and mother. Jesus accused Pharisees and scribes of invalidating the Word of God by their tradition.

That culture and social environment have an immense impact on Christian communities can also be seen in modern contexts. Catholic author W. A. Bailey discusses the shift in Protestant translations of the sixth commandment (Exod. 20:13) from "You shall not kill" to "You shall not murder," which took place to a large degree from the middle of the twentieth century onward, although "You shall not kill" is the preferable translation.[1]

In the New Testament, Jesus broadens the sixth commandment to include even verbal abuse (Matt. 5:21, 22). So, why the change? For Evangelicals, the desire to become mainstream could be part of the reason; for others, the close connection to militarism helped bring about the change. Whatever the reason, the influence of culture led to a change of the wording of the sixth commandment and a change in practice. In a somewhat provocative way, Bailey states, "People want to kill people, and they want biblical permission to do so."[2]

To live in the light does not only mean to acknowledge, confess, and give up one's sin (1 John 1:5–2:2); it also means to obey the Lord's commandments, walk as He walked, and love as He loved (2:3–11). The passage under consideration begins with a statement about knowing God. "Knowing God" and the similar phrases "abiding in Him" (v. 6) and "being in the Light" (v. 9), which are related and refer to the Christian's relationship with God, govern this section of 1 John.

As the second part of chapter 1 contained three false claims, so 1 John 2:3–11 contains also three statements that John has to deal with.

Verses 3, 4	By this we know that . . . The one who says . . .
Verses 5–8	By this we know that . . . The one who says . . .
Verses 9–11	The one who says

Although these verses have a positive thrust, they nevertheless refute ideas that may have been held by John's opponents. Yet the passage is still addressed to all church members, and he wants to encourage them to live a sincere Christian life.[3]

I. KNOWING GOD (1 JOHN 2:3–5)

The section about knowing God starts in a positive way (v. 3). It is contrasted by a negative claim before it turns to the positive attitude again.

Positive:	**We know God, if we keep His commandments.**
Negative:	Who claims to know God and does not keep His commandments is a liar.
Positive:	**Whoever keeps His Word, in him the love of God has been perfected.**

It contains the phrase "keeping His commandments" twice and the phrase "keeping His Word" once. The phrase "keeping His Word" parallels "keeping His Commandments" and is used synonymously.

In verses 3–5 the verb "to know" (*ginskō*) appears four times. This important term is used twenty-five times in 1 John. However, it is not the only Greek verb that means "to know." John uses also *oida* fifteen times in his first letter. It is found in the last verse of the passage we are investigating (v. 11). What are the differences between these two words?

There is some overlap between them. In 1 John 2:29, both are used next to each other and are probably interchangeable. However, there is also a marked difference. While both terms may refer to knowledge as a fact,[4] in 1 John, only *ginōskō* is employed to point to the intimate relationship that humans may have with God when they know Him.

In verse 3, the twofold use of the verb "to know" (*ginōskō*) seems to refer to both knowledge as a fact and knowledge as relation. The perfect tense indicates that people have come to know God, and they still know Him in a personal and experiential way and must grow in this spiritual knowledge. They have a close relationship with Him. The test of such a relationship is keeping the commandments.

The famous noun *gnosis* and the verb *ginōskō* belong to the same word family. Knowledge (*gnosis*) was a crucial term in the religious world of the first centuries A.D. Probably, by the second century, it had developed into a full-fledged heresy called gnosticism, but its beginnings were earlier and can be discerned in texts such as 1 Timothy 6:20 and the Johannine literature. Today some New Age ideas remind us of some of these old gnostic systems. In gnosticism, the emphasis was on mystical experience or esoteric myths about God and self. Salvation was gained through secret knowledge, not through the death of Jesus. Obviously, there was also little concern for moral behavior.[5] John does not use the technical term *gnosis.*

"[I]t is possible that John avoided this term in order to state his message in a manner that could not be misused by his opponents and would not be misunderstood by his readers. . . . Real knowledge of God contains an intellectual, moral, and spiritual component that cannot be separated."[6] Christians must know the Lord, not just know something about Him.

II. KEEPING GOD'S COMMANDMENTS (1 JOHN 2:3–5)

Keeping the commandments is a phrase that occurs quite often in John's writings. In addition, it is found in Proverbs 19:16; Matthew 19:17; 1 Corinthians 7:19; and 1 Timothy 6:14.

What are the commandments John is referring to? Johnson answers by claiming, "In the context of 1 John it can only be faith in Jesus and love for other Christians (1 John 3:23)."[7] In 1 John, the term "commandment" occurs in the singular and in the plural. When John talks about keeping the commandments, he always uses the plural. In addition, the plural is employed in 1 John 5:2: "By this we know that we love the children of God, when we love God and observe His commandments." Here, loving God and keeping the commandments seem to be supplementary but not completely synonymous. *Commandment* in the singular points to love toward God and church members (4:21) as well as faith in Jesus Christ (2:23), something "the secessionists have not kept."[8] The plural may go beyond love and faith in Jesus and include the Ten Commandments. In this context, Smalley talks about the Decalogue and states, "The moral law of God as a whole is represented by the 'orders' (*entolas*) to which John refers, and to which (he says) obedience is necessary."[9] Indeed, indirectly, some of the Ten Commandments are found in 1 John:

Apostasy (2:26; 3:7)	—	first commandment
Murder (3:15)	—	sixth commandment
Lying (1:6, 8; 2:4, 20–22; 4:20)	—	ninth commandment
Lust (2:16)	—	tenth commandment

Keeping the commandments is not a condition for knowing God but a sign that we know God/Jesus and love Him. Therefore, knowledge of God is not just theoretical knowledge but leads to action. The term *Him* may refer to either God the Father or Jesus and is somewhat ambiguous—probably purposely so.[10]

First John 2:4 states the same truth in negative terms and may refer to a false claim made by opponents. Verse 5 repeats verse 3 in more general terms, replaces *commandments* with *word,* and connects love to obedience. "In obedient Christian behavior is manifested a love for God which responds to God's (kind of) love."[11] This is true knowledge of God.

The two phrases *keeping the commandments* (1 John 2:3, 4) and *keeping the word* (1 John 2:5) are somewhat parallel. However, *word* may also be used in a broader sense, including the commandments but moving on to other issues such as believing in the promises of God.[12]

III. WALKING AS JESUS WALKED (1 JOHN 2:6)

The first part of our passage has stressed that walking in the light and knowing God means to be obedient. The second part now calls Christians who want to abide in Him to follow Christ's example.

Abiding, remaining, or *living,* as the term has been translated, stresses the continuity and permanence of our close personal relationship with God "and the need of perseverance on the part of men."[13] It is another important term and is used for us abiding in God (1 John 2:6, 24, 27, 28; 3:6), in the light (2:10), in love (4:16), in the Christian fellowship (2:19), and in the Christian message (2:24). It is also used for God (3:24; 4:12, 15), the Anointing (2:27), God's Word (2:14), the love of God (3:17), and eternal life remaining in us (3:15).

How can Christians walk as Jesus did? First, they have to find out how Jesus lived. Second, on a daily basis they have to compare their conduct to His.

In the context of 1 John, walking as Jesus walked means to love and live for others. Jesus laid down His life for others, and we should be ready to do the same (3:16). Johnson talks about a life "in imitation of Jesus,"[14] and Stott states, "Christian conformity is to the example of Jesus as well as to his commands. . . . We cannot claim to live in him unless we behave like him."[15] This affects our devotional life; our study of God's Word; our struggle with temptations; our behavior at work and in traffic; and our relationship to spouse and children, to neighbors and to people of different nationality, race, and gender, and to our enemies. It influences our attitude toward war and peace, our priorities in life, our input in the local church, our efforts to reach others with the gospel, our habits of spending money, our leisure time, our understanding and handling of ethical issues, and more.

It is always dangerous to separate what the Word of God has kept together. An unbalanced understanding of Jesus can easily lead to an unbalanced Christian life and to false and dangerous doctrines. John accepted Jesus both as Savior and as Lord, and thereby Jesus was his example to follow.

According to 1 John 2:2, Jesus is the Atoning Sacrifice for our sins. In our present passage, the other aspect is dominant. Jesus lived an exemplary life. We should follow His footsteps. Although the death of Jesus and His resurrection are the climax of the Gospels, sufficient information on Jesus' teachings and His life are recorded that we can understand how a human being, ideally, should live. "The test of our religious experience is whether it produces a reflection of the life of Jesus in our daily life; if it fails this elementary test, it is false."[16]

IV. THE NEW COMMANDMENT (1 JOHN 2:7, 8)

After having mentioned the necessity to keep the commandments—plural—in verses 3–5, John turns to *the* commandment in the singular. The discussion on the new commandment and the old commandment that follows seems to be confusing and puzzling.

I am not writing a new commandment to you
But ***an old commandment . . .***
The old commandment is the word . . .
On the other hand, **I am writing a new commandment to you.**

Is John talking about one or two commandments, an old and a new one? Why does he express himself in such a complicated way? What is the commandment? The text seems to suggest that this is only one commandment.

Various reasons are given as to why John sounds so paradoxical. Marshall suggests, "It looks as though they [the opponents] thought that he was putting up some novel rules which they could ignore. This suspicion might have been confirmed in their minds by his talk of a 'new' commandment. . . . So he begins his elucidation of the commandments . . . by emphasizing that the commandment which Christians should obey is not new, but old."[17] Witherington proposes, "Wisdom sayings are full of such deliberate paradoxes. Rhetorically it is meant to impel the audience to listen carefully and think hard: what could be both old and new?"[18]

Verses 7 and 8 do not tell us directly what the nature of the command is. However, the context points to brotherly love. Jesus had earlier used the term "new commandment" (John 13:34). After having showed His disciples what it means to serve (John 13:1–17), Jesus issued His "new commandment." His disciples should love each other just as Jesus had loved them. A similar situation occurs in 1 John 2:6–8. After having talked about walking as Jesus did, John points to Jesus' commandment concerning brotherly and sisterly love.

The commandment of neighborly love was already present in the Old Testament (Lev. 19:18). However, Jesus applied it to His community in a special way. He had lived it during His life and in His death and had fulfilled the law, giving it a depth not known before.[19] And it was the rule for His church. In this sense, it was new. When John wrote his letter, Jesus' "new commandment" had already been a historical reality for many years. In this sense, it was old.

Yet in a sense, this commandment was and still is new. It is new because it is continuously realized in the life of Jesus ("in Him") and His followers ("and in you") in an unprecedented way. "So the new commandment remains new because it belongs to the new age which has been ushered in by the shining of the true light."[20] It is the characteristic of Jesus' eschatological community.[21] Stott lists four additional reasons why the old commandment is still new:[22] (1) There was and is a new emphasis. (2) The commandment was and is new in quality. (3) It was and is new in extent. And (4) its application is always new.

The commandments are summarized in the commandment of love. To walk in the light and to walk as Jesus did means to keep the commandments and love brothers and sisters.

V. LOVING BROTHER AND SISTER (1 JOHN 2:9–11)

The last section of our paragraph begins and ends in a negative way. Verse 9 discusses the claim of someone to be in the light while hating a brother. Such a person is in darkness. Verse 11 returns to hating one's brother. The center, verse 10, shows the positive side—namely, a person loving brother or sister and, therefore, remaining in the light and not stumbling or becoming a stumbling block for others.[23]

v. 9	Who hates his brother is in darkness	—	negative
v. 10	**Who loves his brother lives in the light**	—	*positive*
v. 11	Who hates his brother is in darkness	—	negative

Hate (1 John 2:9, 11) is contrasted with love (v. 10). While 1 John talks about hating the brother four times (2:9, 11; 3:15; 4:20), the author also knows that Christians will be hated by society (3:13). Hating one's brother is a strong statement. We prefer to say that we are irritated or offended, but Scripture oftentimes uses the term *hate* for the same idea, and we should not downplay that aspect of human behavior. *To hate* can refer to literal hate, but it can also mean to despise, to disregard, or to be indifferent.

On the other hand, love is mentioned briefly in verse 5. John dealt with love indirectly in the second part of our passage, the new commandment (vv. 6–9). Love toward fellow Christians is clearly spelled out in the last section of our paragraph (vv. 9–11). First John has much more to say about love. For the moment, it may suffice to note that the term *love* (*agapē*) is employed eighteen times in 1 John. The term *beloved* is found six times. The verb *to love* occurs twenty-eight times. However, the other biblical verb for *to love* (*phileō*), found in the Gospel of John (for example, John 5:20) and Revelation (Rev. 3:19; 22:15), does not occur in 1 John. "This concentration of use marks out the Johannine writings from the rest of the New Testament and other Greek literature of the period. But it is not just the frequency of use that needs to be noted. The Johannine writings, especially 1 John, make love a theological category derived from the action and character of God. On this basis it becomes an ethical category, placing humans under obligation to love."[24]

Why does John talk about love within the church without mentioning love toward our neighbors? In his letter, John is primarily interested in the Christian community. That does not mean he would deny the fact that Christians are called to love their neighbor and even their enemies. But this is not his concern here.

CONCLUSION

Although in life change is normal and even necessary, not all change is desirable and beneficial. Beliefs and practices do not automatically become right simply because they are expressions of ourselves or of the prevalent culture. God's will, as revealed in Scripture, supersedes all human institutions and customs. Therefore, we have to recognize and resist cultural views and practices opposed to the gospel of Christ, lest we damage our relationship to God and water down our message and mission. Then Jesus' words would also apply to us: "Neglecting the commandment of God, you hold to the tradition of men" (Mark 7:8). True Christians will walk as Jesus walked, keep God's commandments, and love not only God but their brothers and sisters as well.

CHAPTER 5

RENOUNCING WORLDLINESS (1 JOHN 2:12–17)

Ted Peters, in his booklet on the stem cell debate, writes, "Some advocates of technoscience are in-your-face, so to speak, about transforming human nature into something beyond nature. . . . Stanley Shostak, for example, would give a neo-naturalist nightmares. He contends that 'a high priority should be placed on manipulating genes, fulfilling biotechnology's potential for creating a healthier and happier humanity.' Going beyond happiness as we have known it, Shostak will stop at nothing short of making people immortal through regenerative gene therapy."[1]

In 1 John 2:12–17, John continues discussing the implication of what it means to walk in the light. He had shown that having fellowship with God leads to a correct attitude toward sin and obedience toward God's commandments. He now stresses our privileges (2:12–14) before he warns against worldliness (2:15, 16). In John, theology and ethics go together, as do biblical teachings and Christian lifestyle. The passage ends with a statement regarding the transient nature of the world. "And the world passeth away, and the lust thereof: but he that doeth the will of God abideth for ever"(2:17, KJV).

This statement flies in the face of Shostak's dream of human immortality and raises many questions. The most crucial one would be, If human immortality would become possible through scientific research, would it be desirable to have our lives prolonged eternally while living under the curse of sin and in this present world with all the violence, crime, greed, corruption, abuse, wars, natural disasters, and so forth?

Renouncing Worldliness (1 John 2:12–17)

John reminds us that this world will pass away but that a wonderful eternal life awaits those who belong to God.

I. The Spiritual Status of Believers—Part 1 (1 John 2:12–14)

First John 2:12–14 deals with the new status of believers, clearly distinguished from the opponents. These three verses consist of two groups of three statements—each addressed to children, fathers, and young people—that are largely parallel.

A. I am writing to you, children (*teknia*),
        because the sins have been forgiven you through His name.
B. **I am writing to you, fathers,**
        because you know Him who has been from the beginning.
C. ***I am writing to you, young men,***
        because you have overcome the evil one.

A'. I have written to you, children (*paidia*),
        because you know the Father.
B'. **I have written to you, fathers,**
        because you know Him who has been from the beginning.
C'. ***I have written to you, young men,***
        because you are strong,
        and the Word of God abides in you,
        you ***have overcome the evil one.***

Unfortunately, in some English Bibles, there is a bit of confusion in verses 13 and 14. The standard Greek New Testaments[2] deal with the first group of statements in verses 12 and 13, and the last group of three statements in verse 14. However, many English Bibles (such as the ESV, the KJV, the NASB, and the NIV) add the first statement of verse 14 to verse 13. On the other hand, versions such as *The New American Bible* (NAB), *The New Jerusalem Bible* (NJB), and the *New Revised Standard Version* (NRSV) follow the verse division of the Greek New Testaments.

Both groups have the same order of addressees—namely children, fathers, and young men. One wonders about the repetition of the same ideas in both sections and the variation of the verb "to write." This repetition is a rhetorical device that underlines the importance of the subject and adds to the liveliness of the passage. It lays the foundation for the next verses: "Only those whose sins are forgiven, who know Jesus and the Father, who have overcome the evil one, who are strong and have the word abiding in them, are able to refuse the love of the world."[3] Sherman and Tuggy add, "By an emphatic reminder of who they are and what God has done for them, he provides the trust basis for exhorting them to live in the victory already won."[4]

It is most natural to understand the children here in the same way as in all the other places in 1 John: the children represent church members in general. The fathers could be those older in faith and more mature, while the young men could refer to those younger in faith. Brown points out that "frequently in NT Greek a plural masculine noun covers subjects of both genders."[5] Therefore, the fathers would include all older church members and the young men the younger church members—male and female. So, their actual age may have been less important than was the time they had been followers of Jesus.

II. The Spiritual Status of Believers—Part 2 (1 John 2:12–14)

In verses 12–14, John stresses three important things relating to the status of believers: (1) their sins have been forgiven, (2) they know Jesus and the Father, and (3) they have remained victorious.

1. Their sins are forgiven

John wants his hearers to have assurance. Referring back to his discussion of sin in 1 John 1:5–2:2, he says that to be a Christian means to have forgiveness of sins.

Genuine Christians do not deny their sinfulness but have accepted salvation through Jesus Christ and, therefore, live with the assurance that their sins have been forgiven. The perfect tense *forgiven* points to an act in the past that has an ongoing effect up to the present. All sins of the past have been *forgiven.* Present sins need to be confessed and will be forgiven as well (1 John 1:9).

"Forgiveness, however, is granted on account of the person and work of Christ on behalf of the believer, not because confession is some magical key that forces God to unlock the treasury of forgiveness. Confession may be seen as a necessary means of receiving forgiveness, but it does not create the divine ability and readiness to forgive."[6]

John says "through His name." The name stands for the person of Christ and His work. The basis of salvation is Jesus and what He has done for us (Acts 4:12). Forgiveness, knowing God, and victory depend on Jesus.

2. They Know Jesus and the Father

While the false teachers claim to know God and Jesus and yet have a false understanding of the divinity and humanity of the Messiah, genuine Christians "know Him who was from the beginning." They "know the Father." The phrase "from the beginning" reminds one of 1 John 1:1 and, therefore, of Jesus Christ. These Christians know both the Father and the Son.[7]

As discussed previously, knowing God has an intellectual aspect, a moral side, and a spiritual component. It is relational. J. I. Packer has pointed out important aspects of the knowledge of God: "If asked how one may know God, we can at once produce the right formula: that we come to know God through Jesus Christ the Lord, in virtue of his cross and mediation, on the basis of his word and promise, by the power of the Holy Spirit, via a personal experience of faith. Yet the gaiety, goodness, and unfetteredness of spirit which are the marks of those who have known God are rare among us. . . . A little knowledge *of* God is worth more than a great deal of knowledge *about* him."

Packer points out what makes it evident that people know God—namely, they have great energy for God, great thoughts of God, great boldness for God, and great contentment in God. He continues, "What were we made for? To know God. What aim should we set ourselves in life? To know God. What is the 'eternal life' that Jesus gives? Knowledge of God. . . . What is the best thing in life, bringing more joy, delight and contentment than anything else? Knowledge of God. . . . What of all the states God ever sees man in, gives God most pleasure? Knowledge of himself. . . . Once you become aware that the main business that you are here for is to know God, most of life's problems fall into place of their own accord."[8]

3. They Have Remained Victorious

Of the twenty-eight occurrences of *overcoming* or *conquering* in the New Testament, twenty-four are found in John's writings. Christians have overcome and will overcome whatever is wrong, including false doctrine, through faith in Christ (1 John 5:5). The victory will ultimately be realized when Jesus comes again.

When the young men are addressed a second time, the phrase "you have overcome the evil one" is repeated, but the statement is expanded: they are spiritually strong and able to resist temptation because the Word of God is the source of their strength. The "Word of God" refers to the divine message revealed in Christ. Akin suggests "that John refers to the Old Testament and to the account of the life of Jesus in his Gospel." And he adds, "The believer's source of strength has not changed. The believer may still overcome . . . the evil one through faith in Jesus Christ and careful study of and abiding in the Word of God."[9]

So Christianity is about forgiveness of sins, knowing the Godhead, and consequent victory. Forgiveness of sins and knowledge of God are characteristics of the new covenant (Jer. 31:31–34; Heb. 8:8–12).[10]

III. Renouncing Any Love of the World (1 John 2:15)

Because believers know God and His Word lives in them, they are ready for the challenge issued in verses 15–17 to not love the world. In verses 15–17, the most frequently used noun is *world* (*kosmos*), occurring six times. In the New Testament, the term *kosmos* designates the universe, the earth, humankind, the realm of existence, the way of life opposed to God, and even adornment (1 Pet. 3:3). However, not all of these shades of meaning are present in 1 John. The world needs salvation, and Jesus has come into the world to be its Savior (1 John 2:2; 4:14). Yet the world is hostile to God and His people (3:13). The world lies in the power of the evil one (5:19). False prophets, antichrists, and deceivers are in the world (4:1, 3; 2 John 7). While it is not wrong to possess the world's goods, these goods should be shared with the needy (1 John 3:17). Finally, the world needs to be overcome (5:4, 5). In the Johannine epistles, the term *world* is predominantly a negative term, because the world is in a state of rebellion against God.

Smalley has provided a helpful outline of verses 15–17:[11]

v. 15	Love of the world	Love of the Father
	↓	↓
v. 16	comes from the world	comes from the Father
	↓	↓
v. 17	the world passes away	the one who obeys God remains forever

In 1 John 2:8–10, love is commanded: Christians must love their brothers and sisters. In 1 John 2:15 love is forbidden: Christians should not love the world. A kind of tension arises when Christians are called to not love the world, while God Himself loved the world (John 3:16). James concurs with 1 John 2:15: "Whoever wishes to be a friend of the world makes himself an enemy of God" (James 4:4). This tension is due to a different shade of meaning of the

term *world* in both contexts. In 1 John 2:15, the term does not mean "the created universe, nor the human race as such . . . but the life of human society as organized under the power of evil."[12]

The reason given in 1 John 2:15 for not loving the world is that God and the hostile *world* are opposed to each other. John does not say we should hate or avoid humans or despise the planet and try to leave the world. But he warns us that whatever we cherish that is in conflict with God prevents us from knowing the love of the Father.

What is the "love of the Father"? The phrase can be understood as the love that belongs to God or as our love for God. It may very well be that John has both in mind. "Authentic love for God and 'worldliness' cannot coexist in the same person at the same time. By this strong antithesis the Elder challenges his readers to purity of life."[13]

IV. PROBLEMS WITH THE WORLD (1 JOHN 2:16)

While verse 15 is quite broad, warning us against loving the world, verse 16 spells out some details. John mentions three things: (1) the lust of the flesh, (2) the lust of the eyes, and (3) the boastful pride of life.

The term translated *lust* can also mean "desire, longing, passion, or covetousness." In the New Testament, it is oftentimes used in a negative way: the desire for things (Mark 4:19), the desire of Satan (John 8:44), and for coveting (Rom. 7:7). In Romans 1:24, Paul mentions the desires of the Gentiles, which include idolatry, homosexuality, greed, envy, murder, strife, and deceit.

Desires can also be positive. Jesus desired to eat the Passover meal with His disciples (Luke 22:15). Paul desired to see the believers in Thessalonica (1 Thess. 2:17), and later to be with the Lord (Phil. 1:23). In Scripture, negative desires are called "evil desire" (Col. 3:5), "foolish and harmful desires" (1 Tim. 6:9), and "ungodly and worldly desires" (Titus 2:12). What John has in mind are, of course, evil desires or cravings.

Dodd suggests that three things are criticized here: sensuality, materialism, and self-glorification.[14] The first temptation has to do with "the lust of the flesh."

1. THE LUST OF THE FLESH

"Flesh" may refer to humans in a neutral way (Luke 3:6): Jesus became flesh (John 1:14). Flesh can also be the physical nature of humans (Matt. 26:41) and can point to human standards (John 8:15), to earthly descent and the human realm of existence (Rom. 1:3), and finally to sinful human nature

(Rom. 7:25; 8:13). It is in the latter sense that it is used in 1 John 2:16.

What, then, is "the lust of the flesh"? The desire of the flesh includes sinful sexual desires, but the phrase is not limited to sinful sexuality. It describes a self-centered approach to life: "the thoughts, decisions, and activities of everyday life are dominated by the cravings of one's own flesh."[15] Marshall includes eating and drinking among the fleshly desires and talks about "the whole nature of sinful man which is comprehended in this phrase."[16]

2. THE LUST OF THE EYES

While the "lust of the flesh" may point to problems arising from our human nature, the "lust of the eyes" may point to external influences, "desire that is aroused by things that can be seen—physical objects, members of the opposite sex, pornographic pictures or images. . . . Visual stimuli in general are envisioned here."[17] But Smalley would go further by stating that sight can be both physical and intellectual, claiming that a blind person could also be affected by the lust of the eyes.[18] By themselves, the eyes are neutral, even innocent, but they can become the means through which evil desires—such as lustful looks and unchastity (Gen. 39:7; Matt. 5:28), covetousness and greed (Josh. 7:21), pride and arrogance (Isa. 5:15)—become ingrained in us.

3. THE BOASTFUL PRIDE OF LIFE

The "boastful pride of life" is the third problem mentioned. In 1 John 3:17, the term *bios,* "life," refers to material possessions, "the world's goods." This may also be the meaning here. People boast in what they have and in what they do. We trumpet around our and our children's achievements, forgetting that all we have and are is from God. We promote ourselves and let people know who we are and what we own. We like to be addressed with ecclesiastical, academic, and professional titles. Humility is a rare virtue today.

Not only do those who love the world boast in their material possessions, they even exploit others. "The opposite of God is greed and exploitation, behaviour which destroys society."[19]

4. NOT FROM THE FATHER

The last part of 1 John 2:16 points out that the hostile world with its evil desires is diametrically opposed to God. The two are incompatible. "Pride, prestige, power, and position count for nothing in the kingdom of God. The value system of this world is turned on its head when God provides the evaluation."[20]

V. THE TRANSIENT NATURE OF THE WORLD (1 JOHN 2:17)

In verse 16, the apostle presented the first reason why we should not love the world: the love of the world and the love of the Father are incompatible. In verse 17, John adds a second reason: It does not make sense to love the world because the world is impermanent. It is better and wiser to choose what lasts.

Nevertheless, although we know that the world is transient, that we are mortal, and that we cannot take anything with us when we die, it still has a magic pull. Therefore, Paul says, "Keep seeking the things above" (Col. 3:1–4) and "We fix our eyes not on what is seen, but on what is unseen. For what is seen is temporary, but what is unseen is eternal" (2 Cor. 4:18, NIV).

In 1 John 2:8, the apostle had already stated that the darkness is passing away. Now he uses the same verb and says that the world is passing away. A new era has already come with the incarnation of Jesus, the Light. The things of this world are passing away. Although for John salvation is both present and future, he is very clear about the fact that there will be an end to the created world. Human history is not cyclical but runs from creation to re-creation.

If it is true that the world is passing away, how can we survive? John answers, by doing the will of God. Although correct theology is important, and John tries to refute the false teachers with their misguided understanding of Jesus and sin, it is also important to live a life of obedience. Our theology must be lived.

Let us not compromise our love for God by an attraction to things and attitudes hostile to God. Culpepper summarizes 1 John 2:12–17 by stating, "Victory is assured, resistance is required."[21]

CONCLUSION

Walking in the light means to turn away from sin and be obedient. Walking in the light also means to be aware of the wonderful privileges that we as Christians have, and therefore we should shun all worldliness. Instead of loving the world, we love God, remembering that this world is passing away.

Dick Rentfro has captured what John shares with us in his first letter: "I cannot afford to become hypnotized by everything I see in the media or the culture—the desire to have the biggest home or the fastest car, while men, women, and children are starving and dying in the world. We should keep remembering that we're here only on *temporary assignment*—pilgrims in a foreign land. . . . God's ideal for us is not material success. In God's eyes, the greatest heroes and heroines of faith are not those with the biggest bank account or those holding political power. Rather it's those who serve faithfully."[22]

CHAPTER 6

Rejecting Antichrists (1 John 2:18–29; 4:1–6)

In March 1997, police found the corpses of thirty-nine people clothed in black and shrouded in purple in a Rancho Santa Fe, California, mansion. The group was part of a cult called Heaven's Gate. Their leader was Marshall Applewhite. They had committed suicide, probably in order to leave this world and join extraterrestrial beings in a UFO, believing that the spaceship was trailing behind the Hale-Bopp comet. Those people were deceived by false teachings and paid with their lives for trusting their leader.

Heresy is not always as bizarre and dangerous as in this case, but it is not to be taken lightly. Throughout history, Christianity has had to wrestle with the problem of false teachings. The struggle seems to intensify as so-called new light travels around the globe in minutes, deceiving multitudes. What aggravates the situation is that supposedly absolute truth does not exist, and each personal conviction—no matter how weird—has become truth. This also means that many people believe that heresy doesn't exist.

Jesus spoke of false christs and false prophets (Matt. 24:5, 11, 24). The apostle Paul warned against "savage wolves" that would attack "the flock" and false teachers from within the church who would draw away church members (Acts 20:29, 30). Second Thessalonians 2 mentions the man of lawlessness (vv. 3, 4) and the mystery of lawlessness (v. 7). Revelation 13 describes a "sea beast" that is an imitation of Jesus that scholars call "the antichrist."[1] First John also refers to antichrists.

I. THE LAST HOUR (1 JOHN 2:18)

1. CONTEXT AND OUTLINE

The statement in 1 John 2:18 that the last hour has come and the previous verse's mention of the fact that the world is passing away may be connected. Smalley states, "Starting from the leading statement of the good news that 'God is light' (1:5–7), John outlines four practical conditions whereby believers may practice and test their own spiritual commitment: by renouncing sin (1:8–2:2), by being obedient (2:3–11), by rejecting worldliness (2:12–17), and [in our present unit of material] by keeping the faith (2:18–29)."[2]

The first part of 1 John 2:18–29 begins with the word "children" (v. 18), which is later followed by the phrase "I have not written to you" (v. 21). It concentrates on the antichrists, who are contrasted with the believers (vv. 18–25). The second part begins with "I have written to you" (v. 26), which is followed by "children" (v. 28). It deals primarily with church members (vv. 26–28).

v. 18	"Children" (*paidia*)
v. 21	"I have not written to you because . . ."
v. 26	"I have written to you . . ."
v. 28	"Children" (*teknia*)

Here is a possible outline of the passage:

Part 1

vv. 18, 19	The last hour and the antichrists
vv. 20, 21	The anointing of the true church members and their knowledge
vv. 22, 23	The error of the antichrists
vv. 24, 25	Church members abiding and having eternal life

Part 2

v. 26	The deceivers (antichrists)
vv. 27, 28	The anointing of the church members and their abiding
v. 29	Ethical implications for church members

2. THE UNIQUE EXPRESSION "LAST HOUR" (1 JOHN 2:18)

Although John had the secessionists in mind right from the beginning of his letter, it is only toward the end of 1 John 2 that he finally speaks about them directly. The secessionists were causing problems for his church members, though evidently they had left the church. Their activity convinces John that "the last hour" has come. This was in the first century A.D.

In the New Testament, the phrase *the last days* (Acts 2:17; Heb. 1:1, 2) and the phrase *last times* (1 Pet. 1:20) are applied to the apostolic age. The incarnation of the Messiah brings "the last days." The entire period between Christ's first and second comings is considered the last days, although the last days have a final segment prior to the Second Coming. Jesus' coming to planet Earth brought the overlap of two ages—the present evil age and the kingdom of God. Now, two seemingly incompatible statements are true: the kingdom of God is already present (as the kingdom of grace), and yet it is future (as the kingdom of glory). We already share in the major benefits of the kingdom, yet we still look forward to its full realization.

John's expression *last hour* is unique in the Bible. When in Revelation 18:8, 10, 17 the judgment of Babylon is described, *day* and *hour* seem to be used interchangeably. Therefore, John's *last hour,* used at the beginning and end of 1 John 2:18, may be similar to the *last days* of other New Testament authors. Witherington writes, "There can be little doubt that our author believes that he and the audience live in the eschatological age or end times already, the last and decisive period of human history."[3]

On the other hand, John may have had in mind the final stage of world history. Jesus had talked about false christs and false prophets, and John may have concluded that the final days had come because he was faced with the antichrists. But John does not set a date for the Second Coming, apparently being well aware of the fact that God's time is not ours (see 2 Pet. 3:8). Stott affirms, "What John wrote was true. And it is still true. The fact that nearly 1,900 years have elapsed since he wrote these words does not invalidate his argument or contradict his affirmation."[4]

It is not wrong to stress the urgency of time. John heeded Jesus' appeal to be awake and ready, and so should Christians in all ages. What we must reject is the setting of dates for Christ's coming.

II. THE COMING OF ANTICHRISTS (1 JOHN 2:18, 19, 22, 23)

The term *antichrist* is used in 1 and 2 John and nowhere else in the Bible. The Greek preposition *anti* means "for," "in place of," "instead of," and "in behalf of." For instance, Matthew 2:22 says that Archelaus was reigning over

Judea *"anti"*—"in place of"—his father Herod. So, is an antichrist someone who takes the place of Christ or someone who is opposed to Christ? The original meaning of *anti* was "opposite," and *anti* as a prefix of a verb or a noun can express the idea of opposition.[5] Stott states, "The early commentators understood the word to signify an 'adversary' of Christ, and if John had meant a 'false' Christ, he probably would have used the term *pseudochristos* as he does *pseudoprophētēs* in 4:1. Certainly the antichrist's teaching is here recognized as being fundamentally against Christ and a denial of Christ (22). Perhaps both ideas are present in the word, 'counterfeiting and opposing' (Plummer)."[6]

Does the antichrist refer (1) to an individual person/system opposed to Christ, or (2) to a group of persons in the sense that there are many antichrists, or (3) to both—various antichrists and *the* antichrist?

The term *antichrist* occurs five times in Scripture. In four of the five references, it is used in the singular.

1 John 2:18	The antichrist is coming.
1 John 2:18	Many antichrists have appeared.
1 John 2:22	The antichrist denies Father and Son.
1 John 4:3	The spirit of the antichrist is coming and is already in the world.
2 John 7	The deceivers do not acknowledge Jesus Christ as coming in the flesh. This is the deceiver and the antichrist.

John seems to craft his language carefully, allowing for multiple antichrists (2:18), while not giving up the idea of one specific antichrist. First John 4:3 talks about the spirit of the antichrist. This means that the antichrists reveal the spirit of *the* antichrist, but the real antichrist has still to be contended with. John "does not deny the future coming of the antichrist."[7] Just as in John's days "the antichrists" were driven by "the spirit of the antichrist" (1 John 4:3) and yet are still called "antichrists," so John expected a manifestation of *the* antichrist in the future (1 John 2:18).

In 1 John 2, the apostle furnishes the following insights on the antichrists:

- Although there is one specific antichrist, there are also a number of minor figures called antichrists (v. 18).
- The antichrists had been members of the church, but a schism happened and they left (v. 19). For John, this was proof that in reality

they never had been part of the church. They "were not authentic Christians."[8] However, John did not call wavering church members antichrists. "Here is one of the clearest expressions in the New Testament of the way in which we must distinguish between the church visible, composed of those who outwardly belong to it, and the church invisible, composed of those whom the Lord knows to be his (2 Tim. 2:19)."[9] This should not discourage church members or lead them to the false conclusion that membership in the church is not important.

- The antichrists apparently claimed superior knowledge and an "advanced" theology, because John tells the church members that it is they and not the secessionists who know the truth and have the Holy Spirit (vv. 20, 21).
- Antichrists are those who deny that Jesus is the Christ and the Son of God (vv. 22, 23). They separate Jesus from God the Father. But John keeps the Father and Son together and mentions both of Them four times in verses 22–24. "If one denies the Son, and if the Father and the Son are an indivisible unity, . . . then to deny Jesus is to deny God."[10]
- Because true Christians accept the biblical-apostolic message—including its correction of theological misconceptions and errors—and because they abide in the Son and the Father, they have eternal life (vv. 24, 25). By implication, the secessionists do not have it. Instead, they will "shrink away from Him in shame at His coming." Biblical doctrines are not dry and irrelevant statements but affect our lives now and in the future.
- Obviously, these antichrists are not involved in practicing righteousness and therefore are not born of Christ (v. 29).

III. TESTING SPIRITS (1 JOHN 4:1–6)

1. SIMILARITIES BETWEEN 1 JOHN 2:18–29 AND 1 JOHN 4:1–6

First John 4:1–6 is another major section in John's first epistle that deals with antichrists. The two passages, 1 John 2:18–29 and 1 John 4:1–6, share a number of commonalities, for instance:

- Both passages deal with the opponents first before concentrating on the character of the Christian church. Apparently, John wanted not only to refute the secessionists but also to anchor his community in the apostolic message and in a personal relationship with God the Father and God the Son.

- First John 4:3, which states that John's audience has *heard* that the antichrist is *coming*, is the closest parallel to 1 John 2:18.
- The "false prophets" of 1 John 4:1 may remind us of the "liar" in 1 John 2:22, because the words have a common Greek root. The false prophets (4:1), antichrist(s) (2:18, 22; 4:3), and deceivers (2:26; 4:6 [the spirit of deception]) seem to be the same group.
- The idea of confessing Jesus is found in both passages (2:23; 4:2, 3).
- Strong contrasts between the true believers and the secessionists occur in both passages.
- Both sections begin and end with true knowledge, which is knowing the truth and knowing God (2:18, 29; 4:1, 6).
- In chapter 2, the antidote to the teachings of the antichrists is (1) the anointment, (2) remaining with the original apostolic proclamation, and (3) doing righteousness (2:27, 29). In chapter 4, it is to be from God and to listen to the apostolic testimony of the church (4:6).

2. THE ANTICHRISTS IN 1 JOHN 4:1–6

The passage 1 John 4:1–6 begins with an important call: Do not believe without testing the prophet and his or her message (v. 1)! The truth is that Christ has come in the flesh and cannot be separated from Jesus. Verses 2 and 3 contain a twofold test—a positive and a negative test. It refers to confessing the preexistence and incarnation of Jesus Christ. Those who do not confess the apostolic message affirmed by the Spirit of truth (v. 6) that Jesus is the Christ and the incarnate Son of God are antichrists.

Obviously, the false teachers claimed to be inspired. That may be a reason why the terms "spirits" and "false prophets" are used to describe them (vv. 1, 3).[11] However, the prophets' erroneous views proved that they were influenced by the spirit of the antichrist (v. 3). The antichrist can be understood as a principle or power rather than an individual person, because the phrase "of which you have heard" (4:3) begins with a neuter instead of a masculine pronoun.[12]

Another problem of the false prophets/antichrists was their involvement with the world, which indicated that they did not belong to God (v. 5). "Though the opponents claim to be God's representatives (1:6; 2:4, 6), the world's values have so permeated their thinking and beliefs that they speak from the viewpoint of the world. . . . Their teaching is popular; it has accommodated to what the world wants to hear."[13]

Although John tells us about the nature of the heresy he had to face, it is not easy to pinpoint a specific historical group. Docetists taught that Christ only seemingly had been a human being but actually was not.[14] Cerinthianism of the second century A.D. suggested that Christ entered the human being Jesus at baptism and left Him before crucifixion so that Christ did not suffer and die. In any case, the opponents John wrote about denied the full humanity of Christ. Therefore, "they are from the world" (v. 5).

While identifying the false teachers that John was dealing with required the criterion of how they related to Christ, other situations may demand additional tests for identifying true prophets, such as agreement with Scripture (Isa. 8:20; Deut. 13:1–3), good fruits (Matt. 7:15, 16, 20), fulfillment of predictions (Deut. 18:22), the absence of a covetous attitude (Mic. 3:9–11), and the proclamation not only of good news but also of unpleasant messages (1 Kings 22). Marshall is certainly right, when he states, "False belief is as much a sin as unrighteous behavior or lack of love."[15]

IV. THE ANOINTING (1 JOHN 2:20, 21, 27)

True believers have received the anointing that remains in them, teaches them, and is without falsehood (1 John 2:20, 27). John wants to reassure church members that they, rather than the antichrists, have the truth. What is said about the anointing and its functions may remind readers of Old Testament accounts and statements, such as the anointing of David and his being filled with the Holy Spirit (1 Sam. 16:13) and the linking of the anointing to the Holy Spirit in Isaiah 61:1. In a special way, it reminded John's audience of Jesus' statements about the Holy Spirit in His farewell speeches (John 14:16, 17; 15:26; 16:7). Jesus was anointed with the Holy Spirit (Acts 10:38). Therefore, it is very likely that "the anointing" stands for the Holy Spirit.

Here we may have a deliberate play on words, because the term *christ* in antichrist and the term *chrism* (anointing) are related. Christ is the Anointed One. The antichrists may claim some sort of anointing or inspiration that gives them special knowledge, but only true believers have the anointing and therefore know the truth (1 John 2:21).[16] This anointing is from the Holy One (2:20). The Holy One may be the Father or the Son. In John 6:69, it is Jesus. In the parallel passage (v. 27), where the anointing occurs again, the context also points to Jesus.

Because of the anointing, the true believers know. There are two manuscript traditions. One reads, "all of you know," while the other one reads, "you know all things." The first option is preferable (see 1 John 3:2).

How should we understand verse 27, in which John says that church members have no need for anyone to teach them while God has given the gift of teaching (1 Cor. 12:28, 29; Eph. 4:11–13) to equip them? We must understand this statement in its context. John's readers knew that Jesus is the Christ who became flesh, died on the cross, rose from the dead, and saved us. John did not need to teach them again. He just had to remind them so that they would not be shaken by the esoteric claims of the adversaries.

However, there is also another dimension. To some extent, 1 John 2:24 is parallel to verse 27:

> "*As for you,* let that abide in you which you heard from the beginning"
> "*As for you,* the anointing which you received from Him abides in you" (NASB).

What the true believers have heard from the beginning is the gospel of Jesus. Furthermore, the Word of God (1 John 2:14) and the truth (2 John 2) abide in the Christian. In 2 Corinthians 1:21, 22, the divine anointing is linked to the sealing with the Holy Spirit, while in Ephesians 1:13, hearing the Word of truth and believing leads to the sealing with the Holy Spirit. Therefore, the anointing may also point to Scripture.

The antidote to the messages of the antichrists is God's Word as communicated by the Holy Spirit. It is the objective standard by which doctrines can be evaluated. Today we can decide to follow Scripture or to espouse nonbiblical teachings of a religious, philosophical, or scientific nature. We can construct our own belief systems based on a conglomeration of current ideas and various traditions and then promote it, or we can choose to accept the biblical message and live it. Our decision will decide whether or not we are true followers of Christ.

V. ABIDING (1 JOHN 2:24, 25, 27, 28)

The two passages 1 John 2:18–29 and 4:1–6 stress that false teachings are as sinful as is false behavior. Some people feel that it is important to exhibit a Christian lifestyle, but they think that doctrines do not matter much and are even divisive. Others stress biblical teachings and live a pagan life. Both acceptance of false doctrines and living a life that does not follow the footsteps of Christ separate us from God and do not allow us to remain in Him.

In 1 John 2:18–29, "abiding"/ "remaining"/"living in" occurs seven times:

Verse 19	The antichrists did not *remain* but left the church.
Verse 24	Believers are called to let the apostolic message *abide* in them.
Verse 24	Condition: if they let the apostolic message *abide* in them
Verse 24	Promise: they will *abide* in the Son and the Father.
Verse 27	The anointing *abides* in genuine Christians.
Verse 27	Believers are called to *abide* in Him.
Verse 28	Believers are called to *abide* in Him.

Verse 19 deals with the secessionists who have left the church. The other references relate to believers. They contain both affirmation and exhortation. Thus, privilege and challenge, promise and call, go together.[17] "There is a direct tie between faithfulness to the gospel and remaining in fellowship with God and God's Son."[18] Christians are called to continue holding on to this intimate relationship with their Creator and Redeemer. One of the effects of remaining in God is to have the wonderful promise of eternal life. Another effect is confidence at Christ's return (1 John 2:28).

While discussing verse 27, Stott challenges us, "Christians should always be 'conservative' in their theology. . . . The continuous obsession for the 'latest ideas' is a mark of the Athenian not the Christian (Acts 17:21). . . . The Christian can never weigh anchor and launch out into the deep of speculative thought. Nor can he forsake the primitive teaching of the apostles for subsequent human tradition."[19]

CONCLUSION

Walking in the light means rejecting all antichrists and false prophets and remaining grounded in the biblical message and in the Father, the Son, and the Holy Spirit. We do not need to end up dead in Rancho Santa Fe, California. We do not need to fall prey to false teachers at either end of the theological spectrum. John has provided tests and safeguards that Christians can follow. They include confession of Jesus Christ incarnate, who died for us and has become our Mediator.

CHAPTER 7

Living as Children of God (1 John 3:1–10)

Some time ago, a boy was born to an unwed mother. Wherever he went, he was asked the same question: "Who is your daddy?" While at school, he would hide at recess and lunchtime from the other students. He avoided going into stores because that question hurt him so badly. He even made a practice of going to church late and slipping out early to avoid hearing the question, "Who is your daddy?"

When this boy was twelve years old, a new preacher came to his church. One day, this new preacher launched into the benediction before the boy realized what was happening, and he got caught and had to walk out with the rest of the congregation.

When he reached the back door, the new preacher, not knowing anything about him, put his hand on his shoulder and asked him, "Son, who is your daddy?" The crowd at the door became deathly quiet. The boy could feel every eye looking at him.

But the new preacher sensed the situation and said, "Wait a minute! I know who you are! I see the family resemblance now. You are a child of God. You have a great inheritance! Go and claim it."

The boy walked out the door a changed person. After that, whenever anybody asked him about his daddy, he would answer, "I am a child of God!"

We are children of God and heirs of His kingdom not through our perfection but because of His grace. In 1 John 3:1–10, the apostle spells out the wonderful privilege of being God's children. Then he moves from our privileges to our responsibilities.

I. THE WONDERFUL PRIVILEGE: CHILDREN OF GOD (1 JOHN 3:1)

1. CONTEXT AND OUTLINE

First John 2:29, a transitional verse, mentions that those who practice righteousness are born of God. They have experienced a new, spiritual birth. This statement prepares readers for 1 John 3:1–10, which focuses on being children of God.

The phrase "children of God" occurs three times in our passage; namely, right at the beginning and at the end (1 John 3:1, 2, 10), encompassing the entire passage. Thus, 1 John 3:1–10 is about being children of God, although other topics are also introduced.

v. 1 We are **children of God.**
v. 2 **Children of God** will be like Him when Jesus comes.
v. 3 Everyone who expects the Second Coming purifies himself.

Expansion:
Part 1 No sinning but righteousness (vv. 4–7)
Part 2 No sinning but righteousness (vv. 8–10)

v. 10 **Children of God** versus children of the devil

First John 3:1–10 contains a number of phrases and individual words that are repeated.

Part 1		*Part 2*	
v. 4	Whoever sins does lawlessness.	v. 8a	The one who sins is from the devil.
v. 5	(Jesus) appeared to take away sins.	v. 8b	The Son of God appeared to destroy the works of the devil.
v. 6	Whoever remains in Him does not sin.	v. 9	Whoever is born of God does not sin.
v. 7	The one who does righteousness is righteous.	v. 10	The one who does not do righteousness is not of God.

For instance, the word family *to be revealed/to appear* and the topics *righteousness* and *sin* occur frequently. There are also significant contrasts, such as God versus the devil, children of God versus children of the devil, and not doing sin versus sinning. And two parallel passages spell out what it means to purify oneself.

2. The Status of Being Children of God

The term *how great* (*potapēn*) in 1 John 3:1 implies astonishment and oftentimes admiration. "The expression carries both a qualitative and quantitative force, 'what glorious, measureless love.' "[1] Stott points out that originally this term meant "of what country" and states, "It is as if the Father's love is so unearthly, so foreign to this world, that John wonders from what country it may come."[2] While previously in 1 John, when the term *love* (*agapē*) appeared (2:5, 15), it referred to our love toward God, now the term describes God's love toward us. God's love consists in loving unlovely creatures and seeking their best. John will dwell on God's love again in chapter 4. God's love has been manifested in calling us His children. The NIV translates 1 John 3:1 freely but catches its meaning well when it says that the Father "lavished" His great love on us. The use of the perfect tense indicates that this amazing love of God is not a one-time event but rather is a permanent gift.

John is especially interested in the fact that believers are already God's children. God has taken the initiative and has worked the new birth. Genuine Christians must know the secret not apparent to nor acknowledged by the world and the secessionists—that they truly are children of God. This implies that the opponents are not children of God but children of the devil (3:10). Since the world and the heretics do not accept Jesus as the Christ and therefore do not know the Father (2:23), they do not know God's children either.

The designation "children of God" does not apply to all humanity. Although all humans are creatures of God, not all of them are children of God who belong to the family of the Divine Father. Not even all who claim to have fellowship with God and to be Christians are God's children. Children of God are those who believe in Jesus Christ as God's incarnate Son and their Savior and Lord (John 1:12), who have experienced a spiritual birth, and who consequently follow Him in obedience, opposition to sin, and a life of love and righteousness.

3. IMPLICATIONS OF BEING CHILDREN OF GOD

- This text contains wonderful assurance. We do not need to worry as long as we maintain our intimate relationship with our heavenly Father.
- From the perspective of space and time, human beings look completely insignificant, so we cannot but be utterly astonished that God is interested in us and makes us His children.
- In difficult situations—for instance, when Christians are shunned, mocked, or persecuted for Christ's sake and feel cut off from God and are tempted to give up their faith—they should remember that being ignored by the world is not necessarily a sign that something is wrong. Difficult circumstances should strengthen, not weaken, our faith. They may be a sign that we are adhering to divine values and are willing to swim against the stream.
- One difference should, however, be kept in mind. In a strict sense, only Jesus is *the* Son of God. Believers do not claim Christ's place.

II. RESULTS AND RESPONSIBILITIES (1 JOHN 3:2, 3)

1. RESULTS

First John 3:2 now portrays the results of this Father-children relationship: we will see Him and will be like Him. Because we recognize our present state as children of God, we also know that the future will be even more marvelous, although we do not yet fully understand it.

The major question is, What does it mean to be like Him? Satan and Eve wanted to be like God (Gen. 3:5; see also Isa. 14:14; Ezek. 28:2). This brought about the Fall in heaven and the fall on earth and introduced sin to the universe. In 1 John, the idea of being like God is introduced as a positive result of being His children.

Satan wanted to be like God in power and probably was not much interested in being like God in character. His desire for likeness with God did not deepen his relationship with God; instead, it was disruptive and ruined that relationship. Eve's case was not much different.

Although Christians will be like God, they do not desire God's place. They want to be like Him in loving others, in selfless service, and in exhibiting purity of thought and righteousness of action. They respect the basic difference between Creator and creature and do not want to eliminate it. For them, the issue is love, not power. They long for Jesus' second coming and a transformed existence.

Although different options are discussed among scholars, there seems to be agreement that being like God refers at least to likeness in character. Johnson notes, "The image of God lost in creation will be restored in Christ as we become like him."[3] Smalley talks about "spiritual unity, but not complete identity."[4] Witherington asserts, "True likeness will be obtained, but not identity with God or Christ."[5] Marshall adds, based on Romans 8:17–19, Philippians 3:21, and Colossians 3:4, that believers will "share his glory," that is, "the process of glorification, already begun here and now in the life of believers (2 Cor. 3:18) will reach completion."[6]

Verse 2 ends with the wonderful promise that believers will see Him as He is. Who is the "Him"? The passage 1 John 3:1–3 introduces God the Father and "Him." It has been suggested that the phrase "He appears" refers to the Son, because the same phrase found in 1 John 2:28 obviously describes Christ's second coming.[7] However, the opinions vary whether "He" and "Him" refer to Jesus or to God the Father. It seems that John is ambiguous and sometimes moves easily from one Person of the Godhead to another without clearly indicating the change. John does not always clearly distinguish between Father and Son because he teaches that Father and Son belong together (2:23).

2. Responsibilities

Because of their hope in Christ's second coming and seeing Him as well as their hope for transformation, children of God purify themselves as Jesus is pure and without sin.[8] Verse 3 is a transition preparing for the development found in verses 4–10. It tells us that true hope leads to a "continual purification process."[9] This process, also called sanctification, consists of cooperation between God and the human being. While in chapter 1, John informs us that the blood of Jesus cleanses from all sin, here he talks about self-purification. We must allow God to do His work in us.

Our example and model is Christ. His absolute pureness inspires us to strive for purity while we expect His second coming. We cannot go on sinning in light of what God has done for us. "We are not to judge our lives by other peoples', but by Christ's, who is the standard or goal toward which we are to move."[10]

III. A Definition of Sin (1 John 3:4, 8a)

The false teachers may have stressed the present blessing of salvation while ignoring the importance of living pure lives. Therefore, John emphasizes that our future depends on how we live now. This has nothing to do with righteousness by works. We are saved by grace alone, but our lives must reflect that we are saved. So, after calling Christians to purify themselves, John goes on to show what that means. To purify oneself means to separate from sin.

In Scripture, sin is described differently, though in complementary ways. The word *sin* (*hamartia*) that John uses typically stands for "missing the mark." "It was used of a warrior who missed striking his opponent or of a traveler who missed the right path."[11] In addition, sin is falsehood, deliberate violation of God's standard of truth, wickedness, disobedience, transgression, trespass, lawlessness, and unrighteousness.

In our passage, sin is defined as lawlessness. As such, it consists of rebellion against God and siding with His enemy.[12] The very next passage, 1 John 3:11–24, relates the story of Cain murdering his brother. This sin comprised a lack of love but also a transgression of the law. Verses 22 and 24 refer to the commandments and emphasize that people must keep them.

Thus, the term *lawlessness* seems to have legal implications. It may remind us of the "man of lawlessness" in 2 Thessalonians 2:3—the antichrist *par excellence*—and of the climax of his activity just prior to the Second Coming. This lawlessness is exhibited by the antichrists in 1 John, who flagrantly rebel against God and align themselves with Satan (1 John 3:8). Church members are indirectly warned in verse 4 to renounce such an attitude and all sin because it is a violation of a personal relationship with God.[13]

Stott drives home the point: "The heretics seem to have taught that to the enlightened Christian questions of morality were a matter of indifference; today our sins are excused either by euphemisms like 'personality problems' or by the plea for cultural relativity."[14] But to ignore sin or excuse it is not a solution. We need to take sin seriously and confront it. The solution to the dilemma of sin is to stay away from it, and, if we sin, to follow 1 John 1:9, where forgiveness is offered freely.

IV. The Appearance of Jesus (1 John 3:5, 8b)

1. Christ's appearance on earth

The term *to appear/to be manifested* is found nine times in 1 John. In most of the cases, it relates to Jesus. In 1 John 1:2; 3:5, 8, it describes His incarnation but points also to His preexistence.[15] According to the second part of 1 John 1:2, Jesus was manifested to the eyewitnesses. In 1 John 2:28; 3:2, the term describes His second coming. In 1 John 2:28, it is parallel to the expression *parousia,* which depicts Jesus' coming. The verb *to appear* is also found in 1 John 2:19 and 4:9.

The antichrists left the church. This manifested that they had not really been part of the church. God's love was also manifested—it appeared in His sending His Son. This passage contains one of the heaviest concentrations of this term in the entire New Testament. Jesus appeared in human flesh, being the incarnate Son. He will appear again at His second coming.

2. THE PURPOSE OF CHRIST'S APPEARANCE

Christ appeared the first time to solve the sin problem (1 John 3:5) and to destroy the works of the devil, who has sinned continuously from the beginning (3:8). Christ has released humanity from subjection to sin, the devil, and death. First John 3:5 does not directly tell us how Jesus took away sins. However, the context of 1 John and of the Gospel of John makes it clear that Jesus did this by dying on the cross.

According to 1 John 3:5, Jesus took away "sins," which may point to sinful actions, the punishment for sin, and the consequences of sin. His substitutionary sacrifice is sufficient for all humanity. The antichrists may not have fully comprehended the salvific value of the Cross. Today, we are again in danger of playing down the role of the Cross. Some make the Cross only a sign of God's love, separating it from the fact that there Jesus died for us. By doing that, they take a soft view of sin and leave "little or no room for the biblical teaching that Christ came not only to demonstrate God's love but to manifest His justice as well."[16] Jesus came to undo all the evil Satan had done in this world and in the universe. This includes the enslavement to sin. "Jesus appeared not merely to do the positive and constructive job of loving, but also to do a demolition job on sin and the works of the devil (1 John 3:8). . . . His death is seen not just as a passive event, atoning for sin, but also as an active attack on darkness. He came not merely to be a sin-bearer, but also a sin-destroyer."[17]

John stresses the absolute sinlessness of Jesus.[18] He says that Jesus *is*—not *was*—without sin. "John's statement is more than the fact that Jesus did not commit sin. He argues that Christ does not possess a sinful nature."[19]

If that is so, and Jesus atones for and eradicates sin, believers cannot have anything to do with sin, "the cancer that eats away at all spiritual life."[20] By making common cause with sin, we would be making common cause with Satan and would be rejecting Jesus.

V. NO SIN! (1 JOHN 3:6, 7, 9, 10)

1. TRUE BELIEVERS CANNOT SIN

Verses 6 and 9 contain strong and perplexing statements saying that no one who lives in Jesus, who has seen Him spiritually, and who has known Him commits sin, and that no one who is born by God sins and or even can sin. How can these statements be reconciled with 1 John 1:6–10; 2:1, 2, where John states that claiming sinlessness is a lie and that although it is the goal of Christians not to sin, they need Jesus Christ as Mediator?

Christians have wrestled with these statements and have tried to find explanations. Some may have fallen into despair because they know that sin is a reality in their lives, even after conversion and baptism. Others have pursued perfectionism. And still others have claimed that their sins are not sins at all.

We can safely assume that the apostle John did not contradict himself. We must understand our present passage in the light of the previous discussion on the topic of sin.

Expositors have crafted different solutions to this difficulty.[21] The most satisfying is the suggestion that John was talking about habitual and persistent sin. The verbs "to sin" and "to do [sin]" are found in the present tense, which points to continuous action. The meaning would be that disciples of Christ cannot continuously sin. They may fall into sin now and then, but they have separated from sin, are opposed to sin, and do not practice a life of sin. The NIV follows this understanding, translating the verbs with the expression "continue to sin." And Akin says, "John is not suggesting that the child of God will not commit a single act of sin. Instead, John is describing a way of life, a character, a prevailing lifestyle. . . . In other words, the believer will not live a life characterized by sin."[22]

The true believer does not continue to sin or "practice sin"—as the NASB translates—because "his [God's] seed abides in him" (v. 9) and he is born of God. God's seed can be understood as (1) God's offspring—namely, a divine principle or the divine nature in the believers,[23] or as (2) that which God has implanted in the person who is born again. In this case, it would refer to the Word of God (James 1:18, 21; 1 Pet. 1:23–25) or "the word which they had heard from the beginning (2:24)"[24] and the Holy Spirit (John 3:6, 8),[25] or both.[26]

2. TRUE BELIEVERS PRACTICE RIGHTEOUSNESS

Both subsections, verses 4–7 and verses 8–10, end with a reference to righteousness. While most of the statements found in 1 John 3:4–10 are somewhat negative, verse 7b is positive. Verse 10 is its negative counterpart, using similar phrases. These two verses mention the righteous deeds of those who follow Jesus. Their righteous acts are a sign of their righteous character. This is what they are to keep concentrating on. True Christianity is not a religious or philosophical system or a mental acceptance of certain truths only; it boils down to the practice of righteousness and love.

CONCLUSION

Followers of Christ must never forget that they are privileged to be children of God and have a wonderful hope that gives meaning to life. Their privileges motivate them to renounce sin completely and practice righteousness—that is, to live a pure life. Although moral purity stems from God because it is He who forgives sins, believers have an active part to play in living godly lives.

CHAPTER 8

LOVING BROTHERS AND SISTERS (1 JOHN 3:11–24; 4:7–5:4)

A calendar contained words to the following effect: Duty without love makes one gruff. Responsibility without love makes one ruthless. Justice without love makes one rigorous. Friendliness without love makes one hypocritical. Intelligence without love makes one cruel. Order without love makes one nitpicky. Honor without love makes one arrogant. Material possessions without love make one stingy. And faith without love makes one fanatical.

True love is much needed these days. Love can change our world, our churches, our families, our marriages, and our relationship with God. In 1 John, the apostle has much to say about love. He devoted three major passages to this subject: 1 John 2:7–11; 3:11–24; and 4:7–5:4, each one building on the previous one.

Witherington notes, "It is an odd but important fact that there is more discussion of love in this little sermon than in any other book in the New Testament. . . . The love discussed is God's holy love for the believers and their love for each other. The love referred to may be unconditionally given, but this does not mean that it does not require a great deal of the recipient. . . . God's love starts with people just as they are but transforms them gradually into the divine likeness."[1]

I. TWO PASSAGES ON LOVE (1 JOHN 3:11–24; 4:7–5:4)

1. SIMILARITIES AND DIFFERENCES BETWEEN THE TWO PASSAGES

Loving Brothers and Sisters (1 John 3:11–24; 4:7–5:4)

First John 3:1–10 ended with the statement that children of God are recognizable because they do what is right and love their brothers and sisters. This statement builds the bridge to the discussion of love in 1 John 3:11–24.

First John 3:11–24 and 1 John 4:7–5:4 are remarkably similar. Both contain the phrase "to love one another" repeatedly (3:11, 23; 4:7, 11, 12). Both warn us against hating our brothers and sisters and stress that they are to be the objects of our love (3:14, 15; 4:20). They emphasize Jesus' and God's self-sacrificial love (3:16; 4:9, 10, 14). Because of this love, life is available for us (3:14; 4:9). To love means also to keep God's commandments (3:22–24; 5:2–3). In addition, many other parallels occur, such as truth, confidence, Jesus as Son of God, faith, abiding, and the Holy Spirit.

In spite of the parallels, the two sections are not identical. While 1 John 3:11–24 focuses on love to one another and uses the word-family *to love* eight times, the second passage employs it thirty-three times and enlarges the topic: we are not only called to love God's children but also God Himself. He loved us first. Most importantly, God *is* love (4:8, 16).

2. An Outline of 1 John 3:11–24

First John 3:11–24 can be subdivided into two sections. The first deals with brotherly love (3:11–18) and the second with confidence and keeping the commandments in the context of love (3:19–24). These two sections are connected by the following words and phrases:

Section 1	***Section 2***
We should love one another (v. 11)	We should love one another (v. 23)
Abiding (vv. 14, 15, 17)	Abiding (v. 24)
By this we know (v. 16)	By this we will know/we know (vv. 19, 24)
Truth (v. 18)	Truth (v. 19)

Marshall notes about the first section, "The nature of brotherly love is illustrated negatively by the contrast with Cain who murdered his brother and positively by the example of Jesus Christ who laid down his own life for us."[2]

An outline of 1 John 3:11–18 follows.

Call: ***We should love one another.*** v. 11

The negative example of Cain and its implications:

Life or death	vv. 12–15
The positive example of Jesus and its implications:	
Laying down one's life, supporting others	vv. 16, 17
Call: ***Let us not love*** with word or tongue, but in deed and truth.	v. 18

First John 3:19–24 begins and ends in a similar way:

By this we will know that we are of the truth.	v. 19
The condemning heart	vv. 19–21
Keeping the commandments	vv. 22–24a
By this we know that we remain in Him.	v. 24

3. An Outline of 1 John 4:7–5:4

First John 4:7–5:4 can be divided as follows:

1. God and love (4:7–10)
2. Love and abiding (4:12–18)
3. Love for God and the brothers (4:19–21)
4. Faith, love, and the commandments (5:1–4)

II. The Definition of Love (1 John 3:11–16; 4:7–16)

1. Love in 1 John 3:11–16

John does not set out to give a lexical definition of love; rather, he shows what love is and what it is not. The example of Cain (1 John 3:12) points out that as he killed his brother, the world—including some people within the church—will hate and persecute the followers of Christ (3:13). Marshall writes that "all hatred is embryonic murder."[3] Therefore, to hate a brother means to be his murderer (3:15). In the Sermon on the Mount, Jesus indicated people transgress the commandment that forbids killing long before they commit homicide (Matt. 5:21, 22).

The word *brother* is used seven times in 1 John 3:11–18. (Sisters are included in this designation.) In verse 12, the brother is Cain's literal brother Abel, but in verse 13, John addresses the church members as "brothers," and all the other references to brothers in this section designate church members. In verse 15, the replacement of the plural with the singular may be intentional. It is easier to claim to love all brothers in general than to avoid hating an individual brother. Maybe we should return to the biblical language within our churches today, and, rather than speaking about Mr. X and Mrs. Y and emphasizing academic and other titles, address each other as brothers and sisters again—at least, if we do not currently use first names. This may reduce artificial distance among us and reinforce the concept that Christians are truly the family of God whose members care for each other and love each other.

John follows the negative example of Cain with the positive example of Jesus (3:16), the supreme demonstration of love. But Jesus is more than an example. The Father sent His Son as an atoning sacrifice. Because of Him, we have already here and now passed from death to life, which is shown by our love for each other (3:14). Love means doing whatever is necessary to help others, even if that requires sacrifice. Love means forgiving and not allowing past mistakes and sins to shape the present and the future. In Jesus' case, love meant giving up His own life. But such an act is meaningful only if the other person benefits from the sacrifice. To use Denney's illustration, if someone jumped into a river and drowned to prove his or her love, it would be quite strange and incomprehensible. But if someone jumped into a river to rescue me from drowning and died in the attempt, that is love.[4] The best definition of love is the character and work of the Godhead as revealed in the plan of salvation.

2. LOVE IN 1 JOHN 4:7–16

Both the first two subsections in 1 John 4:7–16 begin with a kind of call to love each other (4:7, 11, 12). John says that we are commanded to love because love is from God (4:7). But not only is love from God, God Himself *is* love. John makes this remarkable statement that describes the very nature of God twice (4:8, 16). "Only God is completely loving."[5] And, "all true love derives from him. . . . The Gnostics believed that God is immaterial spirit and light, but they never taught that God is love. It is the most comprehensive and sublime of all biblical affirmations about God's being."[6] If it is true that God not only loves but also that His nature is love, then all his actions derive from his love—including His act of judging. "Yet, if his judging is in love, his loving is also in justice."[7]

John then makes the point that if God is love, those who love the brothers and sisters are born of God (4:7). Christian love has its source in the love of God, who has taken the initiative and loves undeserving sinners. There is no love in the biblical sense that ultimately does not come from God (4:7), and human love has constantly to "be redefined and corrected by the divine love because human love in the world has the potential to be corrupted."[8]

The statement that "everyone who loves is born of God and knows God" implies that loving God allows us to understand God better. At the same time, the statement could be misunderstood as if it were saying that we can be reborn by loving. We must interpret this statement in the context of 1 John, in which faith is crucial (see, for example, 1 John 3:23).

God's love was manifested by the sacrifice of His Son. While in chapter 3 the emphasis is on the Son who laid down His life, in chapter 4 the emphasis is on the Father who has sent His well beloved and unique[9] Son into the world. Why? So that we may live through Him (v. 9), so that Jesus can be the Atoning Sacrifice for our sins (v. 10), and so that He can be our Savior (v. 14).

First John 4:11–16 focuses on abiding and love. As God's love was manifested in the life and death of Jesus, so God's love is manifested today in the life of the believers. "The unseen God, who once revealed himself in his Son, now reveals himself in his people, if and when they love one another."[10] To love means to enjoy intimate relationship with God. Here, abiding is for the first time said to be reciprocal: we abide in Him and He in us (4:13, 15, 16). Brotherly and sisterly love and the reception of the Holy Spirit, which allows believers to understand the Father and Son, are signs that God lives in the believers. Love, faith, and abiding in and knowing God are interrelated in this passage and summarized in verse 16.

III. Love in Practice (1 John 3:17–18; 4:19–21)

John is not content to theorize about love. It must be put into practice. We should love not with words but with actions (1 John 3:18). The claim to love the invisible God but not His finite creatures is ridiculous (4:20). Those who make that claim show that for them God is a mere construct of their minds.

According to 1 John 3:18, the apostle rejects loving with words and admonishes to love with works and truth. But we can safely assume that John is not opposed to love expressed with words. How would spouses, children, relatives, and friends feel if they never received a verbal affirmation that they are loved? Encouraging words can provide deep healing of strained relationships at home, in the church, and in the workplace. Even John himself used words to share God's love with others.

However, John is opposed to expressing love only through words while not providing help with people's problems because one does not want to get one's hands dirty. Where it is possible to help with works but people are content to give verbal affirmation only, the word has become worthless. God did not only inform us that He loves us—He sent His Son to die in our place. People who love much do much, because real love is active. Therefore, followers of Jesus are willing to lay down their life for others as Jesus did (3:16) and to use their financial means—literally "the life of the world"—to help brothers and sisters.

Marshall claims that it may be more difficult to provide jobs, food, clothes, a Christian education, a place of refuge, and a home for an orphan than to die for a brother or a sister. "Readiness to lay down one's life is a high ideal, to which we may enthusiastically consent: it is a fairly remote possibility. . . . Meanwhile, however, we are content to live our present comfortable life until that supreme sacrifice is demanded. No, says John, the moment is here now. If you have the means of livelihood in the world . . . *and* you see a brother in want, *and* you show no pity on him, then the love of God cannot possibly be in you. . . . The need of the world is not for heroic acts of martyrdom, but for heroic acts of material sacrifice."[11]

IV. A Crisis of Confidence (1 John 3:19–21; 4:17, 18)

First John 3:19–21 and 4:17, 18 may depict a crisis. In both cases, confidence is lacking and must be restored (3:21; 4:17). John may have encountered church members who were discouraged. Some Christians look at the ideal as portrayed in 1 John and notice that they fall short of God's standard. They still have problems with sin. They do not love enough. They do not feel that they are of the truth (3:19). Or they look at the future day of judgment and are afraid.

The term *confidence* is used four times in 1 John. (The original Greek word can also mean "openness," "frankness," "boldness," and "bold assurance," depending on the context.) The apostle wanted believers to be confident (1) when they approach God in prayer (3:21, 22; 5:14), (2) in view of Christ's coming (2:28), and (3) in regard to the future divine judgment (4:17).

1. The Problem in 1 John 3:19–22

First John 3:19, 20 is difficult to interpret. Some expositors suggest that the heart is accusing believers because they have not lived up to the command to love each other in a practical way. They have hard hearts that rightfully condemn them. The statement that God is greater than their hearts and knows all things is taken as saying that God is even stricter in judgment than their own feelings or consciences and that they need to change their attitudes.[12] "Only if our conscience does not condemn us can we boldly approach God."[13]

The other interpretation holds that 1 John 3:19–21 describes an internal dialogue in a Christian that is taking place in the presence of God (v. 19). While the believer's own heart is condemning him or her—justly or unjustly—God is understood as the final arbiter who can overrule the accusations of the heart (v. 20). Christians should not rely on their feelings but on God and the facts that He has revealed, grasping them by faith. "Listen to what God says about you (you are forgiven, 1:9; you know God, 2:4–6; you know and belong to the truth, 2:20, 21; 3:19; you are the children of God, 3:1, 2, 10; you are loved, 4:10, 11), not to your accusing heart."[14] These interpreters reject the first view because it disregards the purpose of the paragraph and does not provide healing to the wounded heart but increases the problems and consequently does not fit well with a God whose character is love. "The second half of v. 20 is meant as a comfort, not as a threat."[15]

The Christian in view here is not the believer who has committed a major sin "but more often the carefully conscientious one, who is plagued by a sense of guilt and inadequacy."[16] How then is a condemning heart healed? Examine yourself, decide to believe in Jesus, keep God's commandments, and love your brothers and sisters. Entrust yourself to God's judgment, seek Him, and rely on His mercy.

Verse 21 provides a contrast to the previous verses. The uncondemning heart is a heart that does not accuse its owner. It is at rest or has been pacified. With such a heart, the believer has confidence and unrestricted fellowship with the Lord. Therefore, morbid self-condemnation should be replaced by confidence in a God who has loved us and saved us, who hears our prayers (3:22), and with whom we may live in a love relationship.

2. THE PROBLEM IN 1 JOHN 4:17, 18

First John 4:17, 18 is related to the passage we have just considered. Here again, the issue is confidence. Verses 17 and 18 form contrasts. While verse 17 portrays a positive picture, verse 18 shows the other side, thereby sharpening and further clarifying the issue.

Love is brought to completion with us.	v. 17a
We have confidence on the day of judgment.	v. 17b
In love is no fear.	v. 18a
Love is not brought to completion in the fearful.	v. 18b

Believers can choose between confidence and fear. One excludes the other, and love triumphs over fear. The mutual abiding of God and believers (v. 16) leads to love, and love leads to fearlessness in the day of judgment. Believers are encouraged to follow the example of Jesus, in whom love reached its goal and fear was banished. Although we must respect God, we cannot approach Him in love while hiding from Him in fear.[17] Love leads to confidence and fearlessness.

V. LOVE AND THE COMMANDMENTS (1 JOHN 3:22–24; 4:21–5:4)

Both 1 John 3:22–24 and 4:21–5:4 end with a reference to the commandments. The term *commandment* is used four times in each section and is associated with love. First John 5:2 talks about "doing the commandments."

First John 3:22, 24 and 5:3 use the famous phrase "keep the commandments." John insists that keeping God's commandments and doing what pleases Him give Christians confidence that God hears their prayers (3:22). Keeping the commandments allows for mutual abiding—we in God and God in us—and the gift of the Holy Spirit (3:24). Loving God means keeping the commandments, and indeed they can be kept because they are not burdensome (5:3).[18]

The references to the commandment(s) in our passages provide the following insights:

- Keeping the commandments may be parallel to doing what pleases God and may, therefore, be understood quite generally (3:22), pointing to moral righteousness in individuals.
- It is God's commandment to believe in Jesus as the Messiah (3:23). This was a problem for the antichrists.
- It is also God's commandment to love each other (3:23). Faith in the name—that is the person, character, and authority of Jesus—and love go together.
- By switching from "the commandment" in the singular to "the commandments" in the plural, John may indicate that the one commandment of love expresses itself in a multiplicity of commandments.
- "The condition of Christ dwelling in us and of our dwelling in him is this comprehensive obedience (24a), and the evidence of the indwelling is the gift of the Spirit (24b)."[19]
- In John's writings, obedience to God's commandments has nothing to do with legalism. It is Jesus' atoning sacrifice that provides forgiveness of sins (2:2).

- In 1 John, the commandment to love includes not only brothers and sisters but also God Himself (4:21; 5:2).
- Although Jewish regulations may have been a burden, God's commandments are not (5:2). This verse reminds us of Jesus' own statement in Matthew 11:30. "It is the will of an all-wise, all-loving Father who seeks our highest welfare."[20]

When Jesus was asked which of the commandments is the most important, He pointed to the commandment to love God with all one's heart, soul, mind, and strength and to love the neighbor as oneself (Mark 12:28–31). Yet He also stressed that those who love Him keep His commandments (John 14:15). In the Johannine writings and in Jesus' theology, love and commandments are connected. The commandment is to love God and others, and to love is to keep the commandments. Love does not make obsolete the keeping of the commandments; rather, it requires that we observe them.

Both John and Jesus had a very positive view of the commandments, and so should those who follow Jesus. Marshall states, "The Christian is to be a person who obeys the commandments (2:3) and pleases God, just as Jesus always did what pleased God (Jn. 8:29). . . . The more fully we enter into that relationship, the more will our asking be in accordance with his will."[21]

CONCLUSION

Love is not just the way in which God deals with His creation, it is His nature. Love is self-giving, seeks the best of others, and benefits them. It forgives mistakes and is creative and highly active. Christians follow the example of love set by Christ and God the Father by loving their spiritual family and, by implication, all human beings.

CHAPTER 9

Believing in the Son of God (1 John 5:1–12)

Ideas about who Jesus was varied in antiquity, and they vary today. Some scholars separate the biblical Jesus from the so-called historical Jesus and claim that the two may not have had much in common. They say the historical Jesus was a common man with a stronger sensitivity for the divine than other humans have. He was not raised from the dead.

Heinz Zahrnt is one example among many who have a low view of Jesus. In his opinion, Jesus may never have called Himself "Son of God," and it may be better to talk about "Jesus of Nazareth" rather than "Jesus Christ." He believes that Scripture describes the death of Christ in many contradictory images that are no longer intellectually acceptable. When talking about the resurrection of Jesus, people make a statement of faith, he claims, not a factual statement.[1]

Others follow an understanding of Jesus as portrayed in certain New Testament Apocrypha and other esoteric traditions; for example, the gnostic Gospel of Judas. We still remember the hype that arose with the publication of the book *The Da Vinci Code,* which claimed that Jesus had a relationship and a child with Mary Magdalene.

The way we think about Jesus dramatically influences how we relate to God, how we understand the plan of salvation, and whether we have assurance of our salvation.

I. BELIEVING IN JESUS AND VICTORY (1 JOHN 5:1–5)

1. STRUCTURE AND CONTEXT

The first five verses of 1 John 5 describe those who are born again. John wants his audience to believe in Jesus as the Christ. Those who do are born of God. They also love God and one another and keep God's commandments. Those who believe Jesus is the Son of God overcome the world (5:4).

In verses 6–9, John deals with the witness about Jesus Christ. He shows the identity of this Jesus in whom he wants people to believe, and he provides support for his claim.

The last three verses of the chapter point to the results or consequences of the witness about Jesus. Faith in Jesus—in God's testimony about His Son—results in eternal life.

Although it may look as though verses 1–5 do not have much in common with verses 6–12, they are linked through Christological designations. These designations are of special importance in 1 John because the antichrists were challenging the beliefs that Jesus and Christ were identical and that the human Jesus was the divine Son of God. Just as anti-Trinitarian sentiments upset believers today, so in the days of John the antichrists shook the confidence of church members. No wonder John felt compelled to address this issue again and again, even when he was dealing with other topics.

An Outline of 1 John 5

<u>vv. 1–5</u>	**1. The character of those born of God**
v. 1	*Believing that Jesus is the Christ*
v. 1	<u>Being born of God</u>
v. 2	• They love the children of God
vv. 2, 3	• They keep the commandments
v. 4	<u>Being born of God</u>
vv. 4, 5	• They overcome the world
v. 5	*Believing that Jesus is the Son of God*
<u>vv. 6–9</u>	**2. The nature of the witness**
v. 6	Jesus came
	by WATER AND BLOOD,
	THE SPIRIT testifies
vv. 7, 8	The testimony of

	THE SPIRIT
	WATER AND BLOOD
v. 9	The reliability of the witness of God
vv. 10–12	**3. The results of the witness**
v. 10	Testimony and faith
vv. 11, 12	Testimony and life

2. THE CHARACTER OF THE REBORN

In 1 John 5:1, the apostle begins with a general principle: Those who truly believe that Jesus is the Christ and exhibit true love are born of Christ. They love the One who begat/has born them as well as the one who is born of Him. Modern translations often render the phrase this way: "whoever loves the Father loves the child born of Him" (NASB).[2] This is not a literal translation because neither *Father/parent* nor *child* are found in the Greek text. However, the meaning seems to be captured well. The "child" is not Jesus but the believer who is born again and loved by fellow believers. "Whoever has been begotten of God naturally loves him who begat him,"[3] and "those who authentically love the one who begat (God) also love the one who has been begotten (one's brother or sister in Christ)."[4]

The last phrase of verse 1 prepares the reader for the next verses' statements on love toward God and His children and on keeping the commandments. Stott reminds us that "love for God is not an emotional experience so much as a moral commitment."[5]

First John 5:4, 5 focus on conquering the world. In order to conquer the world, one must be born again and have faith. To be born again is a supernatural event by which the person is taken from the realm of the world and added to the family of God. The kind of faith that is needed to overcome is defined at the end of verse 5, faith that Jesus is the Son of God.

Throughout history, some people have come to believe that the battle Christians have to fight is an actual battle. This is a disastrous misunderstanding. Nowhere in Scripture are Christians called to set out as crusaders and convert others by force. Nowhere in the New Testament is a nation to be equated with the kingdom of God. The battle that Christians have to fight is a spiritual battle. In none of the apostle John's writings does he say that violence and physical force are the means of overcoming. Rather, Christians overcome by faith, and faith is exhibited by acts of love.

The Conqueror *par excellence* is Jesus Christ. Because He has won the victory, His followers can—according to John's Gospel—experience peace and take courage in the midst of tribulations (John 16:33). They also can overcome and, in fact, have already overcome (1 John 4:4). In Revelation 12:11, overcoming is linked to the sacrificial death of Jesus. In other places in Revelation, the overcomers receive wonderful promises—for instance, access to the tree of life, which signifies eternal life (Rev. 2:7), protection from the second death, that is, eternal death (Rev. 2:11), preservation of their name in the book of life (Rev. 3:5), and participation in Christ's rule (Rev. 3:21). "To believe that Jesus has been victorious is to have the power that enables us also to win the battle, for we know that our foe is already defeated and therefore powerless. . . . It requires a firm belief in Jesus to enable us to dismiss this appearance of irresistible, uncontrollable evil as being merely appearance."[6]

What has to be overcome? Moral pressures from society and from our sinful nature, intellectual challenges such as heresy, and physical problems, including persecution. "Confidence in the divine-human person of Jesus is the one weapon against which neither the error, nor the evil, nor the force of the world can prevail."[7]

II. The Jesus in Whom We Believe (1 John 5:6–8)

John now goes on to show his audience who this Son of God was. He states that Jesus came "by water and blood."[8] Three major interpretations have been suggested: (1) the phrase refers to the sacraments of baptism and the Lord's Supper; (2) the phrase alludes to the blood and water coming out of Christ's body after He died; and (3) the phrase refers to Jesus' baptism and death.[9]

The sacramental understanding has problems, because the verb "to come" used in the aorist describes a historical event in the past, while sacraments are observed recurrently. Furthermore, in the New Testament, blood by itself is not employed as a symbol of or allusion to the Lord's Supper.

The phrase "blood and water" is used in John 19:34 in connection with Jesus' death, but obviously it is not referring to the water that John mentions in 1 John 5:6–8. First, the phrase appears in reverse order. Second, in John 19:34, blood and water comprise a single witness because the two terms refer to the unitary—although separated—blood of a dead person. However, in 1 John 5:7, 8, water and blood are two separate witnesses.

The third explanation of water and blood is the most satisfying one. In

John's Gospel, water is associated with baptism (John 1:26, 31, 33; 3:5, 23). This seems to be the setting for 1 John also. Jesus came as the incarnate Lord and began His public ministry by being baptized with water. He more or less ended His earthly ministry when, on the cross, He shed His blood. Apparently, *water* points to Jesus' baptism and *blood* to His death on the cross (1 John 1:7). Jesus' baptism and crucifixion revealed who He was. In both cases, divine manifestations and human reactions showed that He was indeed the Son of God (Matt. 3:17; 27:50–54).[10]

The secessionists did not deny that the man Jesus was baptized and died, but they didn't assign salvific importance to these events. If Jesus was neither the Messiah nor the Son of God, if the Son of God had left the human being Jesus before His crucifixion, the message would be that the atoning death of the Son of God is not necessary for our salvation. The Son of God did not die on the cross in our place in order to redeem us. Salvation would be through knowledge (*gnosis*) and not through the Cross. "As soon as we reduce the death of Jesus to that of a mere man, so soon do we lose the cardinal point of the New Testament doctrine of atonement, that *God* was in Christ reconciling the world to himself."[11]

So, blood and water were two witnesses. And John adds a third witness—the Holy Spirit, who is truth. He speaks of the Holy Spirit in the present tense. This fact may point to the ongoing ministry of the Holy Spirit as He testifies about Jesus. He may do this in an objective way through the Word and in a subjective way through the inward experience of believers.

In verse 8, the three witnesses of verse 6 are named in almost reverse order. The Holy Spirit comes first. Jesus had announced that the Holy Spirit would testify about Him (John 15:26). Then follows water and blood. These three witnesses agree with each other, while the testimony of the false witnesses at Jesus' trial was inconsistent. Why are these witnesses needed? In the Old Testament, two to three witnesses were required to confirm a matter (Deut. 19:15). John makes it clear that the case regarding Jesus has a sound foundation.

For John, the idea of witnesses or various testimonies about Jesus is quite important. In his Gospel, he mentions several others: John the Baptist's testimony (John 1:6, 7), Jesus' own testimony (3:32), the testimony of the Samaritan woman (4:39), the testimony of Jesus' works (5:36), the testimony of Scripture (5:39), the testimony of God the Father (8:18), the testimony of the people who watched the resurrection of Lazarus (12:17), the testimony of the

Holy Spirit (15:26), and the testimony of the apostle John himself (21:24). John establishes that belief in Jesus rests on powerful testimonies.[12]

III. Jesus and the Testimony of God (1 John 5:9, 10)

While verses 6–9 discuss the nature of the witness, namely the threefold witness of water, blood, and Holy Spirit and the witness of God, verses 10–12 portray the results of this witness, namely faith and life.

What is this testimony of God John cites in verse 9? People have understood the testimony of the Father in our text in different ways.[13] It seems to make most sense if we take it as referring to the threefold testimony mentioned in the preceding verses. God's part is to testify about Jesus. Our part is to believe in Him.

Indeed, oftentimes we take at face value what people tell us, what we find in the newspaper, and what the news on the TV tells us. Seldom do we question whether or not the information is reliable. We are willing to believe. How much more willingly should we accept God's own witness and believe in Jesus as portrayed in the New Testament. God is reliable and true (1 John 5:20). If we do not accept His testimony, we are saying that God is a liar, and this is a very serious accusation. At the end, we will stand self-condemned. "Unbelief is not a misfortune to be pitied; it is a sin to be deplored. Its sinfulness lies in the fact that it contradicts the word of the one true God and thus attributes falsehood to him."[14]

IV. The Issue of the Trinity (1 John 5:7, 8)

Verse 7 contains an expansion, called the Johannine Comma, that was added centuries after the New Testament canon was in place. Instead of reading, "For there are three that testify" and then going on with verse 8, where the three witnesses are mentioned, the verse was enlarged by an addition to read (as in the NKJV): "For there are three that bear witness in heaven: the Father, the Word, and the Holy Spirit; and these three are one."

With this addition to verse 7, the Three Witnesses of verse 8 were now lacking Their introduction, so another insertion was necessary: "And there are three that bear witness on earth." Consequently, the text then proclaimed three heavenly witnesses and three earthly witnesses, the latter being the Spirit, the water, and the blood.

Many biblical scholars agree that this statement is not genuine and was added, possibly to support the doctrine of the Trinity. The additions are found in older Latin Bibles, and from there they seem to have crept into Greek manuscripts. However, they are not found in any Greek manuscript that is older than the fourteenth century A.D. In other words, in Greek manuscripts of the New Testament, the added words are found only in some relatively recent ones.

Stott summarizes the consensus among scholars: "The words occur in no Greek MS [manuscript] before the fourteenth century (except one eleventh-century and one twelfth-century MS, in which they have been added in the margin by a much later hand); in no quotation by the early Greek fathers, who, if they had known the text, would surely have quoted it in their Trinitarian debates; and in none of the ancient versions (translations), even the early editions of the Vulgate. They first appeared in a fourth-century Latin treatise, after which some Latin fathers began to quote them. They found their way into the AV because Erasmus reluctantly included them in the third edition of his text."[15] *The Seventh-day Adventist Bible Commentary* states, "The disputed words have been widely used in support of the doctrine of the Trinity, but, in view of such overwhelming evidence against their authenticity, their support is valueless and should not be used."[16]

In addition, this insertion does not make much sense because it has the "Word," which is Jesus, testifying about Jesus. Furthermore, an addition to the biblical text such as the one found in 1 John 5:7, 8a is not needed because the concept of the Trinity is strongly established elsewhere in John's writings. Not only does John make powerful statements on the divinity of Jesus (John 1:1–3, 14; 8:58, 59; 10:30, 31; 20:28), he also places the Son next to the Father (for example, 1 John 2:23; Rev. 3:21), ascribes to the Son divine titles that belong to the Father (for example, Rev. 1:8; 22:13), and supports worship of both the Father and the Son (Rev. 5:8–14). Although the authors of the New Testament believe that God is One, they portray Jesus and the Holy Spirit as God. The concept of the Trinity is crucial to reconciling the oneness of God with the divinity of the Father, Son, and Holy Spirit. Returning to our passage, in 1 John 5:1–12, the apostle was not trying to establish the doctrine of the Trinity. He wrote this passage to bolster faith in Jesus as the Son of God and to present the witness about Him.

What disturbs us most here is the tampering with the biblical text against which, for instance, Revelation 22:18, 19 warns us. Although the Johannine Comma is an exception rather than the rule, inserting extraneous material into the biblical text threatens to result in far more damage than gain. It may lead people to doubt the reliability of Scripture and mistrust God's Word. They may mistakenly claim that the doctrine of the Trinity has no biblical support or may even give up any faith in God, throwing out the baby with the bath water. There is no need to do so. Scripture is reliable, and in this case, the problem has been solved.

V. The Result of Believing in Jesus (1 John 5:11, 12)

God has provided a wonderful gift for humanity. This gift is eternal life (1 John 5:11, 12), and it is available only in Jesus Christ. We receive it by accepting God's testimony about His Son—in other words, by believing in Jesus.

John's discussion on faith in Jesus and who Jesus is and why we can accept God's testimony has a clear practical goal—namely, that we find eternal life in the Son of God. John's opponents have a different Jesus and do not believe in the true Jesus in the biblical sense. Therefore, they do not have eternal life. Even if they claimed to possess eternal life, even if they had "superior knowledge" and had a good feeling about having eternal life, their claims would not be true.

John clearly states that those who do not have the Son of God do not have life, while those who have Jesus have everlasting life. This would imply that people who have not accepted Jesus do not have eternal life and—if they pass away—cannot live on in heaven, in purgatory, or hell. That eternal life does not mean that a part of us survives death is clear from John 6:54. Eternal life is already a present reality in the sense that true believers have a new quality of life here and now (John 10:10) and live with the assurance that at Jesus' second coming, He will resurrect them from what the Bible calls "sleep." These people will live with the Godhead forever.

Conclusion

It is crucial to believe in Jesus as taught in Scripture and proclaimed by the apostolic eyewitnesses. God testifies to who Jesus is, and only this Jesus can give us eternal life. Faith in Jesus must be an informed faith. We cannot pick and choose but have to accept God's testimony about Jesus Christ, God's Son, in order to receive the benefits—namely God's wonderful gift of everlasting life. Believing in Jesus also means truly loving God and His children, keeping His commandments, and obtaining victory over the world.

CHAPTER 10

CONFIDENCE (1 JOHN 5:13–21)

Our world is full of uncertainties. We do not know how secure our jobs are. We are not protected against fatal illnesses, attacks by terrorists, wars, or disasters. Human life is very fragile. We do not know what our marital and family life will be like ten years from now, and sometimes we are not sure about our relationship to God.

Yet we crave certainty, so we try to establish a certain level of security. We formulate prenuptial agreements. We buy insurance. We lay aside money for the education of our children. We have regular medical checkups, and we plan for our retirement. How, then, can we live without assurance regarding our relationship with God? Living with Him forever is more important than anything in this world. The last passage of 1 John deals with the concept of confidence, ending this letter on a positive note.

I. HAVING CONFIDENCE (1 JOHN 5:13–21)

1. STRUCTURE AND CONTEXT

At the end of his first letter, John presents a wonderful message of assurance and confidence. First John 5:14 contains the word *confidence*—a word we have encountered before. Although *confidence* appears just once in this final passage, the concept is not limited to this term. Another way John expresses the idea is by the repeated use of the phrase "we know."

In addition to the overarching theme of confidence, we find other emphases in this last part of 1 John. Verse 13 speaks about "the Son of God" and "eternal life." This is repeated in verse 20, creating an inclusion that encompasses the entire passage.

The last verse of the letter, 1 John 5:21, does not contain any greetings, reminding us of the introduction, which also lacked both greetings and references to the author and the recipients. It contains an imperative.

Eternal Life

- Confidence about having **eternal life** through faith in the Son of God — v. 13

Two Kinds of Prayers

- Confidence that our petitions will be answered, if they are according to God's will — vv. 14, 15
- Confidence that our intercessory petitions will be answered, if they refer to SIN not leading to death — vv. 16, 17

Three Affirmations

- ***We know*** that those born of God are preserved from SIN and *the evil one* by the One born of God. — v. 18
- ***We know*** that we are of God. — v. 19
- ***We know*** that through the Son we know God and are in Him, **the Eternal Life.** — v. 20

Exhortation

- A call to guard oneself from idols — v. 21

In 1 John 5:13, the apostle writes *you know* and writes about assurance of salvation. From 5:15 onward, he uses *we know.* We can be confident that our prayers are heard (vv. 14, 15). In 5:18, "we know" is followed by the promise of divine protection. In 5:19, the same phrase, "we know," introduces the wonderful concept of belonging to God, and 5:20 stresses that "we know" Jesus' ministry, and thereby God, and are in Him. Therefore, Christians have confidence with regard to their relationship to God, their prayer life, and their present state and future destiny.

The beginning and end of 1 John correspond. In both passages, Jesus is called "His Son Jesus Christ" (1:3; 5:20), probably to refute the antichrists. Both passages portray the problem of sin as very important (1:7–2:2; 5:16–18). And both passages contain the concept of life (1:1, 2; 5:13, 16, 20).

II. HAVING ETERNAL LIFE (1 JOHN 5:13)

Verses 11 and 12 of chapter 5 refer to the assurance of salvation. However, 1 John 5:13 goes further than those two verses. It states an important reason why John decided to write this letter: he wanted his readers to have the assurance of salvation. He wanted them to know that they already *have* eternal life as a present reality. The present tense underlines the continuous possession of eternal life. The condition for receiving eternal life is to believe in Jesus as the Son of God.

Verse 13 surpasses other New Testament texts dealing with everlasting life. These mention a condition and contain a promise (for example, John 3:36), but 1 John 5:13 states that God wants us to have the assurance of salvation. "If God's revealed purpose is not only that we should hear, believe and live, but also that we should know, presumptuousness lies in doubting his word, not in trusting it."[1]

Some Christians subscribe to the motto "Once saved, always saved." Others—knowing that isn't true; one can lose the crown that one already has (Rev. 3:11)—doubt that one can have assurance of salvation. Both groups err. The Bible teaches that there is assurance of salvation, but we can lose this certainty through our own choices. We need to hold on to Jesus Christ and daily surrender our lives to Him in repentance, faith, and obedience. As Johnson points out, there is "the need for continuing faith on the part of those who are already Christians."[2] We must know that we are saved.

III. PRAYERS BEING ANSWERED (1 JOHN 5:14–17)

1. PETITIONS

After having stressed assurance of salvation, John turns to confidence with regard to our prayers. If we ask God for anything that is according to His will, He will hear us favorably.[3] At the same time, we have the confidence that we have already received what we have been praying for.

We can come to God with all our joys, burdens, and requests. We can tell Him that we need money, have problems with our children, or are seriously ill and need His intervention. Do we know that He will send us a check, straighten out our children, or heal us? Not necessarily. Not even Jesus was delivered from tasting death on the cross. That means that we do not directly know all of God's will for us. We may bring our petitions to Him anyway, but we should add to our prayer "Your will be done" and trust that the Lord will do what is best.

However, in other areas of our lives, God's will is crystal clear because it is defined in Scripture. If we confess our sins and ask for forgiveness, God does not put us on a waiting list. If we ask Him to make us His children, God will answer such a prayer right away. Whenever the will of God is revealed in Scripture—whether in a commandment or a promise—and we claim that expression of His will, we know that the prayer is answered. First John 5:14, 15 addresses such prayers. Johnson notes, "The Elder says *we have* (not 'we will have') *what we asked* him for. The realization of our prayer has already begun when we have asked in faith for something . . . that is God's will for us."[4]

If we have any need that is covered by God's commands or promises—for instance, freedom from worries (1 Pet. 5:7), the gift of the Holy Spirit (Luke 11:13), wisdom (James 1:5), the ability to love our enemies (Matt. 5:44)—we may ask God for what we need, refer to His promise in 1 John 5:14, 15, and thank Him for answering our prayer. We do not rely on our feelings, but trust in Him (Rom. 1:17; Heb. 11:6).

Of prayer that claims God promises, Ellen G. White wrote, "There is a condition to this promise,—that we pray according to the will of God. But it is the will of God to cleanse us from sin, to make us His children, and to enable us to live a holy life. So we may ask for these blessings, and believe that we receive them, and thank God that we *have* received them."[5]

2. INTERCESSION

Some observations on 1 John 5:16, 17 are in order.

- John's focus is on intercessory prayer for brothers and sisters who are sinning. The issue is that we help each other. Instead of spreading rumors, we are called to pray for each other. "The way to deal with sin in the congregation is to pray."[6]
- "Sin leading to death" is mentioned in passing and is not the main emphasis of verses 16, 17. Death may not refer to physical death. Rather, it has been suggested that this sin may mean " 'tending in direction of' or 'leading to' spiritual death."[7]
- All sin is unrighteousness and cannot be justified or tolerated (v. 17). It is always dangerous and should not be played with. In the end, all sin leads to death (Rom. 6:23).
- John does not prohibit prayer for those who have committed "sin leading to death." He just seems to say that such prayer cannot be prayed with the same confidence.
- The phrase "he will ask, and He will give him life" should be understood in such a way that the second personal pronoun "He" refers to

> God, not to the person engaged in prayer. "In 1 John 1 it is God who forgives and restores."[8]

We do not know precisely what John had in mind when he differentiated between sin leading to death and sin not leading to death. His original audience must have known. Today there are basically three suggestions of how to understand "sin leading to death":[9]

1. Some suggest that John is dealing with a specific, deadly sin, distinguishing "between what later came to be called 'mortal' (deadly) and 'venial' (non-deadly) sins."[10] Although the Old Testament distinguishes between certain types of sins, the context in 1 John does not favor such an approach. Marshall adds, "Let it be plainly said that if there were no forgiveness for deliberate sins, then we would all be under God's condemnation, for which of us has not sinned deliberately since our conversion and new birth?"[11]
2. "Sin leading to death" is the unpardonable sin that Jesus mentioned—blasphemy of the Holy Spirit (Matt. 12:31, 32). "This sin, committed by the Pharisees, was a deliberate, open-eyed rejection of known truth. They ascribed the mighty works of Jesus, evidently done 'by the Spirit of God' (Mt. 12:28), to the agency of Beelzebub."[12] It is a persistent sin, not an act of sin. John may refer to this specific type of sin.
3. The third option is apostasy. The false teachers had completely rejected Jesus and remained in their deliberate rejection. They did not accept Him as Christ and Son of God. They had also separated themselves from the church. Hebrews 6:4–6 may shed light on 1 John 5:16, 17.

Many expositors favor the third option.[13] However, a combination of options 2 and 3 may be possible.

Can true Christians commit the sin of apostasy, or is people's apostasy an indication that they were not true Christians to start with? Stott and Akin believe that apostasy is "not a possibility" for true Christians.[14] Other scholars challenge this position,[15] and we would agree with them. Some church members may have been tempted to accept the teachings of the antichrists. Therefore, the statement about sin at the end of 1 John contains an element of warning. "The fact that John needed to warn his readers against the possibility of sinning and failing to continue in the truth and in the doctrine of Christ

(2:24; 2 Jn. 7–11) suggests that he did not altogether exclude the possibility that a person might fall away from his faith into apostasy."[16] Church members should pray for each other "lest any of their number should cross the line that leads to open and deliberate rejection of the way of life."[17]

However, if sinners repent and return to God, their sin will be forgiven (1 John 1:7, 9). Jesus prayed for Peter before he denied Him (Luke 22:32), and Peter was restored later on. Witherington states "that no human being infallibly knows the state of another person's heart and faith. Thus it is right to err on the side of mercy, if err we must, and assume that 'where there is life, there is hope' for any sinner."[18] In other words, we should pray for others even in the case of apostasy. We may, however, not be able to pray with the same confidence in all cases.

Not only do these verses encourage us to be confident when interceding for others, they also call us to be more concerned about the spiritual welfare of our Christian brothers and sisters and to pray more consistently and earnestly for them.

IV. Confidence of Being Protected (1 John 5:18, 19)

In 1 John 5:18–20, John writes "we know" three times. Each verse begins with these two words. However, John is not concerned with knowledge only. These verses express confidence and also contain indirect challenges.

Verse 18 concerns every true believer. The statement is a follow-up to the problem of sin mentioned in 1 John 5:16, 17. The person born of God does not keep on sinning. The phrase "born of God" is repeated in the second line of verse 18, but different readings follow in the Greek manuscripts of the New Testament and, therefore, also in our translations. Some manuscripts use the personal pronoun "him," while others use the reflexive pronoun "himself."

Using the Reflexive Pronoun

"We know that whoever is born of God does not sin;
but he who has been born of God keeps **himself,**
and the evil one does not touch him."

Using the Personal Pronoun

"We know that whoever is born of God does not sin;
but He who has been born of God keeps **him,**
and the evil one does not touch him."

In the first case, people who are born again keep themselves. This statement is an indirect admonition only. In the second case, Jesus keeps the believers. Now we are not talking about an indirect admonition only—namely, that we are not to sin—but also a statement that offers great confidence. The latter is a promise that we are in Jesus' hands and that He will take care of us if we do not let go of Him.

Which reading is to be preferred? Most New Testament scholars would argue for the second reading.[19]

1. Although a great number of Greek manuscripts, most of them more recent ones, support the first case, important early manuscripts, as well as the Latin Vulgate, support the second reading.[20]
2. The context of 1 John 5:18 is clearly one dealing with assurance and confidence. In such a context, the second reading is the stronger one and makes more sense.
3. The second reading makes sense on grammatical grounds. Greek uses different participles for the two English phrases "the one born of God." The first phrase occurs in the perfect tense and may describe the lasting effect of regeneration in the believer. The second participle occurs in the aorist, which refers to one specific event in the past. Here it describes Jesus' incarnation.[21] The usage of the same term for Jesus and His disciples may point to the fact that Jesus has become one of us. But "the writer has changed his verb tenses to make clear the distinction between the Christian . . . and Christ."[22]
4. In the Johannine literature, the verb *to keep* is used thirty-six times. Quite often it refers to keeping God's Word and the commandments, but in a number of cases, God and Jesus do the "keeping" (compare John 17:11, 12, 15; Rev. 3:10). Understanding 1 John 5:18 as a promise that Jesus keeps God's children is very much in line with these statements as well as with Jesus' promise that no one will snatch His sheep out of His hands.

The last part of verse 18 stresses that the evil one does not "touch the believer to the point of doing harm to him."[23] This is not an automatic assurance but "a reality made possible . . . so long as we choose to be open to the transforming impact of God's love and to live from it."[24]

The evil one is mentioned again in verse 19. The dative of "evil" can be either masculine or neuter, in the latter case pointing to an evil power rather than an evil being. However, since in verse 18 the evil one is masculine, describing Satan, it is evident that verse 19 also points to the devil. First John 5:18, 19 provide a short glimpse at the great controversy between Christ and Satan. Johnson calls it "the cosmic moral battle between Christ . . . and Satan."[25] This controversy is spelled out in more detail in the book of Revelation.

In verses 18, 19, John refers to the world as the arena of the evil one. While the entire world is, literally translated, "in the evil one"—that is, "in his grip and under his control . . . quietly lying . . . in the embrace of Satan"[26]—true Christians can be confident because they belong to God and He is protecting them.

V. Having True Knowledge of the Godhead (1 John 5:20, 21)

Here John states "we know" a third time. The Son of God has come into this world and has revealed God the Father to us. This knowledge not only is superior to the "knowledge" of the secessionists but also leads to a close connection with God.

Who is the true God according to 1 John 5:20? Some exegetes suggest God the Father.[27] Many opt for the Son.[28] The arguments in favor of the Son seem to be stronger. Throughout his first letter, John switches easily from the Father to Jesus. In some cases, the personal pronouns *He* and *Him* may even refer to both Father and Son. John used the word *true* three times in 1 John 5:20. The first reference may point to God the Father.[29] The second reference seems to refer to Jesus: "We are in Him who is true, in His Son Jesus Christ." The last part of this clause seems to explain the first: The Son of God is the One who is true. The third time the term *true* occurs in this verse is in the line "This is the true God and eternal life."

Here are some arguments in favor of seeing Jesus as the true God:

- The closest antecedent to "This is the true God" is "His Son Jesus Christ." Although Stott sees "the true God" as referring to the Father, he admits, "grammatically speaking, it would normally refer to the nearest preceding subject, namely *his Son Jesus Christ.*"[30]
- Although the term *true* is an attribute of the Father (John 7:28; 17:3), it is more frequently used to describe Jesus (John 1:9; 6:32; 15:1; 1 John 2:8; Rev. 3:7, 14).
- In the Johannine writings, Jesus is God (for example, John 1:1, 18; 8:58; 20:28; Rev. 5).
- This true God is "eternal life." Life is associated with Christ (for example, John 1:4; 11:25; 14:6; 1 John 5:12). According to 1 John 1:1, 2, Jesus

is the Word of life, the Life, and the Eternal Life. By calling Jesus the "Eternal Life" at the beginning and the end of 1 John, the apostle would be creating an inclusion.

- "Finally, it is more likely that the Elder would end his exhortation with a resounding affirmation of the full deity of the human Jesus, the key truth denied by the secessionists' false teachers, and with the assertion, against them, that to know this Jesus is to have eternal life itself (compare 5:11–13)."[31]

The Gospel of John begins and ends by calling Jesus God (John 1:1 and 20:28). The same approach seems to be used in 1 John (1 John 1:1–3 and 1 John 5:20). Thus the Gospel of John and the first letter of John climax in the declaration that Jesus is God and that eternal life is found in Him.[32]

To this point in his first letter, John has not mentioned idolatry. Instead, he wrestled with false concepts of Jesus and their influence on those church members who had not left the church. Why would John, as a final admonition at the very end of his letter, introduce a topic not found before? Obviously, he considered false views of Christ to be idolatry. Since the sin leading to death is a rejection of Jesus as the Son of God, so idolatry is associated with the antichrists' teachings about God and Jesus. Their understanding of the Godhead must be seen as worship of false gods.

The concluding verses of 1 John are not a "mere afterthought or epilogue. They are the christological conclusion toward which our author has been driving. . . . We have here the ultimate amplification; if the significance of Jesus was not perfectly clear before, here it is made apparent: he is God. The coupling of this verse with the next in effect amounts to . . . saying: 'Choose this day which God you will believe and serve.' "[33]

CONCLUSION

John finishes his first letter on a very positive note. Although he warns us against false teachings and the resultant lifestyle, he devotes the last paragraph of his letter to telling us that we can be confident. Christians do not need to live with fear, uncertainty, and doubt. On the contrary, God wants us to be confident regarding the important areas of our life. When we have the Son of God, we have assurance of salvation, confidence that our prayers are answered, and certainty about our relationship with God.

CHAPTER 11

IMPORTANT THEMES IN 1 JOHN

After the Great Disappointment in October 1844, many who had expected Jesus' second coming were perplexed when seemingly nothing happened. Some concluded that Jesus must have returned invisibly. However, if Jesus had come again and had established His kingdom of glory, sin should also have been done away with forever. Consequently, people living in God's kingdom of glory on the present planet Earth would no longer be able to sin. If this reasoning were true and sin would no longer exist, an immoral lifestyle would have nothing to do with sin. People could kill their children, cheat society, commit adultery, and oppress the disadvantaged and it wouldn't matter. This false theological belief would lead to a decadent lifestyle with horrendous consequences. What we believe, then, does matter—it influences how we live.

John introduced a number of different themes in his first letter and came back to them repeatedly. Some of the major themes are false teachings about who Jesus is, sin, love, confidence, being born of God, obedience, abiding, and the Holy Spirit. We will take a brief look at some of the important themes in 1 John—namely, John's understanding of the Godhead, what he teaches about the church, what salvation and abiding is all about, and what we can expect for the future.

I. THE GODHEAD

First John deals extensively with Jesus and, therefore, with the Godhead. As already discussed, a major problem of John's opponents was the issue of who Jesus is and how He relates to God the Father. John stresses the humanity of

Christ and His sacrificial death. "Unlike the gospel prologue, where the emphasis lies on the eternal unity between the unique Son and his Father, here the Elder emphasizes the humanity of the 'Word of life' by speaking graphically of Jesus' physical reality."[1] Yet he makes it very clear that having the Son means having the Father, and denying the Son means denying the Father (1 John 2:23, 24). We will not return to this controversy now but will take a positive look at what the epistle says about the Godhead.

John deals with the nature of the Godhead and portrays God's relationship to humanity. He mentions Father, Son, and Holy Spirit (1:2; 2:24–27). The main emphasis is on Jesus and the Father. The letter tells us that God is light and that darkness, that is, evil, is not found in Him (1:5), God is righteous (2:1), God is love (4:8), and He is true (5:20). Our ability to love is dependent on the God who is love (4:7–12, 16, 19). God's relationship with the believers is expressed in that we are called His "children" (3:2), and He is portrayed as our Father. Father, Son, and Holy Spirit take special interest in each of us and care for us (3:21–24).

John also informs us about what God has done for us and is doing for us now. The letter refers to Christ's incarnation and His death, which is clearly salvific. The incarnate Son of God, Jesus, has taken away our sins (3:5) through His substitutionary death (2:2). Thielman writes, "When Jesus died, he atoned for sin because his death substituted for the death that sinners deserved. He was the climactic and final Day of Atonement sacrifice."[2] At the same time, He has come to defeat the works of the devil (3:8). The Cross and the blood of Jesus save us, nothing else (4:9, 10). Presently, Jesus serves as our Advocate (2:1). God forgives our sins, cleanses us (1:9), and gives us eternal life (5:11). He offers us assurance and confidence (5:14). The work and focus of the Holy Spirit is Christ-centered, confessing Jesus (2:27). As a consequence of our relationship with God, we live as Jesus lived, love as He loved, keep His commandments, and abide in Him.

Abiding is a major term in 1 John, pointing to the fully reciprocal relationship between God and believers. They abide in God and God abides in them. F. Matera suggests that "the central theological issue of 1 John . . . is *koinonia,* which is often translated as 'fellowship' but is better rendered 'communion.' For whereas fellowship suggests a social relationship between two parties, the *koinonia* of which John speaks is participation in a shared reality (the life of God) whereby believers are in communion with one another. . . . Communion with God, then, is participation in the life of God."[3]

II. THE CHURCH

The term *church* (*ekklēsia*) is found neither in 1 John nor in 2 John nor in the Gospel of John. It occurs in 3 John 6, 9, 10, and in the book of Revelation. Nor are church offices mentioned.[4] Nevertheless, 1 John deals with the church. The topic of communion points to the church.

In the New Testament, the church is presented through a number of images, such as salt (Matt. 5:13), pillar (1 Tim. 3:15), temple (1 Cor. 3:16, 17), bride (Rev. 21:2), and body (Eph. 1:22, 23). In 1 John, the church is primarily portrayed as a family (2:9–14, 18; 3:1). There is the heavenly Father (twelve times). In addition, John is a kind of father figure. The church members are children (thirteen times), fathers and young men (each twice), and brothers (thirteen times). John addresses them as the "beloved" (2:7). These terms imply a close relationship to and love for each other and contain the notion of belonging together. Everyone is needed and everyone has a place in God's family. This community has a horizontal dimension and a vertical dimension.

This concept is further expressed through the term *fellowship* (1:6, 7) and the personal pronouns *we* and *you*. In addition, the "issues of authority, right belief and the boundaries of the community" that are "at the centre of 2 and 3 John"[5] are also found in 1 John. There is and must be a distinction between the world and the church (2:15–17). The church is devoted to God; therefore, its members are children of God. Those who are part of the world are children of the devil. There are some clearly defined boundaries.

There is also a difference between orthodoxy—the message they received from the apostles and eyewitnesses (1:1–3)—and heresy as proclaimed by the secessionists (2:22; 4:1–3). John also differentiates between orthopraxy, on the one hand, and a life devoid of love and the keeping of God's commandments on the other. What the antichrists believed about Christ and the life they lived was not in harmony with the church's understanding of Jesus Christ and Christian ethics. So there are "insiders" and "outsiders." Although there is some latitude, the church has boundaries when it comes to biblical doctrines. The false teachers of 1 John had left the church but were threatening its existence by trying to win faithful church members to their theology. The survival of the church was at stake.

John confirms that the church has the right knowledge and doctrine (2:18, 29; 4:6) and confesses the true Christ (2:23; 4:2, 6). Lieu maintains that "the testing of statements of faith in the light of tradition and experience is the task and responsibility of the whole community of faith."[6]

Although the term *unity* does not appear in 1 John, unity is one of its themes. False teachings threaten the unity of the church and must be addressed. In some cases, this may necessitate separation from those who hold fast to positions that contradict Scripture.

III. SALVATION

The verb *to save* is not found in 1 John. Nevertheless, salvation is clearly spelled out. John confesses Jesus as the "Savior" (4:14). If we need a savior, it is evident that we are lost without such a person. We are sinners and subject to death (3:14).

John takes sin very seriously (see 5:16, 17). He does not brush it away as the false teachers have done with their teaching "that the one who has been spiritually enlightened may attain a perfection that places him beyond temptation and sin."[7] Instead, John says that "not even the most mature Christian can attain sinless perfection in this life"[8] (see 1:8, 10). Denial of sinfulness or refusal to call misbehavior sin does not solve the problem. But while John maintains this position, he does not want Christians to take a soft approach to sin. Sin must be recognized and confessed, and the Christian ideal is and remains full victory over sin (2:1). In fact, in what sounds like a contradiction, John says, "The one who practices sin is of the devil . . . ; whoever has been born of God does not sin" (3:8, 9).

In the face of these surprising statements, one should not forget that Paul's writings contain the same tension. He states that we have died to sin (Rom. 6:2, 11) and yet calls us not to sin (Rom. 6:12). "Because the present age overlaps with the age to come, sin is still a possibility for believers. . . . The Elder apparently expects his readers to allow each statement to qualify the other. He thus leaves the total impression with his readers that the one who knows God will want to keep his commands and yet will sometimes sin. Because sin is still a possibility, confession and forgiveness are also necessary. . . . Christians must admit that they sin, and Christians must not sin. There is a tension here, but it is ultimately the same tension that lies beneath the ethical teaching of much of the New Testament."[9] The secessionists do not understand the full extent of sin and therefore have a problem with Jesus' atoning death and His role as our Advocate.

How then does 1 John portray our salvation? We are saved by believing in Jesus as the Christ and Son of God (3:23; 4:15; 5:1, 5), confessing our sins, which are forgiven through Jesus' blood (1:7, 9; 2:2), and being born again. This leads us to hate sin and love God and His children. The means of our salvation is Christ's blood (1:7; 5:6, 8), His atoning sacrifice (2:2; 4:10). First John does not mention the Cross directly. However, blood and atoning sacrifice point unmistakably to the Cross. It is not the example of Jesus that saves us. It is His death. His example calls us to walk as He did (2:6).

Salvation is also described in terms of eternal life. The noun *life* is found thirteen times in 1 John. Jesus is the Life (1:1, 2; 5:20). He promised eternal life to us (2:25). This life is already a reality for those who have the Son (5:11, 12). Christians must even have the assurance that they have eternal life (5:13), and yet they always depend on the sacrifice and the mediating work of Jesus, who is their Advocate.

For John, salvation of the believers is already a present reality, although he does not deny a future dimension. He describes it in various ways:

- Believers have come to know Him (2:2, 3).
- They are in Him (2:5; 5:20).
- Their sins have been forgiven (2:12).
- They have overcome the evil one (2:13, 14; 4:4).
- They have passed from death to life (3:14).
- They are from God (4:4, 6; 5:19).
- They have eternal life (5:12, 13).

IV. Ethical Behavior

Guthrie notes that "there is a surprising lack of specific ethical instruction in this epistle. It rather sets out principles than precepts. The believer is expected to know the difference between light and darkness."[10] This observation does not deny that 1 John contains strong ethical concerns. Although in this letter John deals with erroneous theology, he again and again moves to ethics. Theology informs ethics. The apostle insists "that in the life of the community belief and behaviour are inseparable from one another."[11] "There is no separation between faith and praxis."[12] We cannot think wrong ideas and concepts and act morally. Our thought processes will affect our lives. Therefore, we must make sure that our theology is truly biblical and correctly translates into practice.

It is saddening to see how "good Christians" defend orthodoxy but run away with their neighbor's wife or husband. It is tragic when church members cheat and mistreat each other. John makes a number of statements dealing with moral behavior. He calls Christians not to sin (1 John 2:1) but to walk in the light (1:7), not to lie (1:6; 2:21), not to kill nor to hate brother or sister (3:15), not to love the world with its lusts and boastful pride (2:15, 16), and not to practice lawlessness (3:4). Positively, he tells them to be obedient (5:2), to do what is right (3:7), and to love God (5:1) and each other in a tangible way (3:17, 18; 4:7; 5:1).

Although Paul is more detailed than John when it comes to ethical demands,[13] John has summarized them in the command to love God and fellow Christians and in the call to keep God's commandments and to walk as Jesus walked (2:6). "In attempting to sum up the ethical approach of this epistle, we note first the dominant factor of love (*agapē*). It may be said to be the most characteristic feature in the writer's theology. Yet nowhere is it assumed that the Christian can work up his own brand of love. It is essentially a derivative of the love of God."[14] "John highlights a new dimension of love: its origin in God."[15] Believers demonstrate this love by remaining in the Christian community and sharing their wealth with those who are in need. The apostle also connects love with keeping the commandments. "The link between love and commandment prevents the latter from being approached in a legalistic way."[16] Jesus is the chief example of what love should look like.[17]

Today, people suggest that what is right or wrong is not a matter of absolutes; rather, it is ever-changing, depending on circumstances, culture, and the demands of society. However, John is convinced that there are absolutes. God's will revealed centuries ago is still the norm. Therefore, it is not true that everything is relative or that situation ethics is a good option for Christians.

In 1 John, we notice a sharp contrast between truth and falsehood. John knows that truth exists. God is true. Jesus and the Holy Spirit are truth (4:6; 5:20). Believers "belong to the truth" (3:19). On the other hand, there are liars, who, for instance, deny that Jesus is the Christ. However, sincere Christians know the truth, love in truth, and belong to the truth. Truth is both what we intellectually grasp and what we practice. This concept is important for us today. It warns us against self-deception and pride and encourages us to live the truth and accept the existence of absolute truth.

V. FUTURE EVENTS

In his first letter, John does not have much to say about last-day events. The hope of Christians is already to a large degree realized. They are children of God and have eternal life. Lieu says, "Life, knowledge, victory, strength are 'eschatological' realities; elsewhere in the New Testament they belong in full to the final defeat of evil and realisation of God's kingdom. For 1 John they are part of the community's present experience and a key to their confidence."[18]

In this respect, 1 John resembles John's Gospel. Jesus' long speech about His coming, the signs of the times, and readiness on our part as found in the Synoptic Gospels is missing in the Gospel of John. Instead, there are only short glimpses dealing with the future resurrection (John 5:28, 29) and the preparation of places for us that will be available after the Second Coming (14:1–3). It seems that John has reserved for the book of Revelation most of what he has to say about final events.

Yet 1 John has some statements that point to the future. John seems to be convinced that he lives in the last hour (1 John 2:18). This last hour may encompass the time between Christ's first and second comings, pointing also to the future events that John is expecting. Ladd suggests that John believes in "an imminent parousia."[19]

The last hour is associated with the coming of antichrists. These antichrists point to a specific antichrist at the end of the age. The special antichrist is described in more details in texts such as 2 Thessalonians 2 and Revelation 13.[20] These texts contain a future dimension that seems to be implied in 1 John.

The apostle is convinced that Jesus will come again. The Second Coming should find believers prepared (1 John 2:28; 3:2, 3). They can expect the day of Christ's return with confidence, and they can be unashamed if they abide in Jesus.

Jesus' return will allow believers to see Him (3:2). A kind of transformation will apparently happen in conjunction with the Second Coming, because God's children will be like Him. The hope mentioned in 1 John 3:3 refers to the appearance of the Lord in the previous verse.

Finally, John talks about the day of judgment in conjunction with Christ's second coming. He says we do not need to fear it. Because God loves us and we love Him and His children, fear is inappropriate. While we rejoice at what is already ours, we look forward to the glorious event of His appearance.

CONCLUSION

We need 1 John very much today because of the biblical testimony it gives regarding the nature of Christ, which is again being questioned. Erroneous old ideas are being brushed up and sold again. John warns his readers and us not to believe everyone and not to uncritically accept new doctrines but to test whether or not a teaching is truly biblical. He says we need the discernment to distinguish truth from error. According to John, authentic Christianity has these marks: (1) belief in Jesus as the Son of God who has come in the flesh, (2) observance of the commandments of God, and (3) love toward God and toward our brothers and sisters. John wants to lay a solid foundation and help his audience to have assurance of salvation through faith in Jesus Christ as proclaimed in Scripture.

John's Letter to the Chosen Lady (2 John)

Postmodernism is a philosophy of life that many people today have accepted. To follow the axioms of postmodernism, one has to espouse pluralism and relativism and give up any notion of absolute truth. Pluralism postulates that all views are equal and that all religions lead to god, whoever or whatever that is. According to relativism, there is no absolute truth. Nothing is certain. Nobody can claim to have found *the* truth. Some have concluded that unchangeable truth and timeless doctrinal meaning are human inventions that contradict reality.

It must be admitted that human reason is fallible and that bringing together the various teachings of Scripture in a coherent whole results in a preliminary picture because as humans we have only a partial picture of reality. However, this fact is not to deny that there is absolute truth, that definite statements of belief can be made, and that the partial picture of God and His plan of salvation that we have is true. While theological thinking must be marked by humility, it should not deny that there is truth and there is error and that correct biblical teachings can be distinguished from heresy. This was obviously the position John took in his second letter. In that letter, *truth* is an important term.

John's second letter resembles 1 John in many respects. However, in contrast to the first letter, the second one is clearly cast in a letter form with a formal introduction and conclusion. The main body of the letter contains praise, an exhortation to love and to walk according to the commandments, and a section dealing with the antichrists. Second John does not return to the same subject repeatedly in the kind of circular way that 1 John does; rather, it is more straightforward. At the end of 2 John, the elder expresses his wish to see his audience soon and have a direct encounter with his church members. An outline of 2 John follows:

vv. 1–3	Introduction
vv. 4–11	Message
v. 4	Praise for faithfulness
vv. 5, 6	Exhortation to continue in love
vv. 7–11	Warning against false teachers
vv. 12, 13	Conclusion

I. WALKING IN THE TRUTH (2 JOHN 1–4)

1. THE ELECT LADY

In 2 John, the apostle addresses a lady and her children. The term used for *lady* does not simply refer to a woman in general; it is the female form of the term *lord.* This word occurs again in verse 5. At the very end of the epistle, we read about the children of her sister. Interpreters have understood the elect lady in verse 1 (1) as a woman—an individual unnamed person; a lady named Electa;[1] Mary, the mother of Jesus; or Martha, which in Aramaic means "lady";[2] or (2) as a church.[3]

If one accepts the first option, one must understand the lady, her children, and her sister as literal persons. In the second case, the "lady" represents a church and its members. Johnson expresses the opinion of many Bible students: "The chosen lady and her children is the author's way of referring to a church and its members."[4] And even a cursory reading of 2 John seems to support this view, suggesting that the letter is addressed to a group of believers. Obviously, these believers are mature Christians and not literal children. First Peter 5:13 contains a statement similar to 2 John 1, also apparently referring to a local church. Furthermore, in other places in the New Testament, the church is portrayed as a woman (for example, Eph. 5:22–32; Rev. 12:1–6). Marshall thinks that the term may refer to the church as "the bride of the Lord" (Rev. 19:7; 21:9).[5]

2. LOVE AND TRUTH

Second John uses important key words. In the beginning, it employs the terms *truth* and *love.* Later, *truth* is replaced by the term *commandment.* In verses 9 and 10, *teaching* becomes important.

Truth and *love* are combined in verses 1 and 3, and indirectly in verse 4 because the commandment mentioned in the latter verse may refer to faith in

Jesus Christ and love for each other (compare 1 John 3:23). In verse 5, the commandment is explained as love for each other. "But even Christian love can be counterfeited by people who present the appearance without the reality. So the elder adds that he loves 'in truth' " (v. 1).[6] Love can be interpreted in a purely emotional way and even in a sensual and superficial way. Christian love is true love—love expressed in the context of truth. The emphasis on love and truth indicates that John's churches are facing a crisis that has to do with love and especially truth.

In verse 2, truth seems to be personified. Truth remains in us and will be with us forever. Truth reminds us of Jesus, who is *the* Truth (John 14:6), and of the Holy Spirit. As the Holy Spirit is with the believers forever (John 14:16), so truth is with them forever (2 John 2). Both truth and love ultimately point back to God and belong together. They form the main theme of 2 John. We need truth so that we can discern deceptions and their results (vv. 7, 8) and abide in the teaching of Christ (vv. 9, 10).

Second John 3 is a promise or affirmation rather than a mere wish. Grace, mercy, and peace come from both God the Father and Jesus. Father and Son are placed next to each Other. This statement prepares the way for another statement linking those Two Persons of the Godhead (v. 9) and for the discussion of the problem with the antichrists (v. 7), who obviously denied the divinity of Jesus and the true humanity of Christ. The truth is that Jesus Christ is the Son of God. Believers walk in the truth (v. 4).

Stott declares, "Our love for others is not to undermine our loyalty to the truth. On the other hand, we must never champion the truth in a harsh or bitter spirit. . . . So the Christian fellowship should be marked equally by love and truth, and we are to avoid the extremism which pursues either at the expense of the other. Our love grows soft if it is not strengthened by truth, and our truth hard if it is not softened by love."[7]

II. WALKING ACCORDING TO THE COMMANDMENTS (2 JOHN 4–6)

It is encouraging for church members to hear that their spiritual leader rejoices greatly that they "walk in the truth" (v. 4). It motivates them to continue their Christian life "in truth just as the Father has commanded" them. But although in verse 4 John expresses his joy that "some of your children [are] walking in truth," he thereby also admits that some of them are not. Either a schism has already taken place or is about to happen.

After the rejoicing (v. 4) comes a request that is also an exhortation (vv. 5, 6), the first of three. John again talks about a commandment (v. 5)—namely, that we are to love one another. Witherington suggests, "In the wake of the schism, the audience must maintain the bond of love with the author and the church."[8] The commandment is not a new command. "They must, however, embrace it even more intensely and reject those things that counteract the commandment: the reception of error or falsehood, which causes schism."[9]

In verse 6, John shows that love means keeping God's commandments. It is not just what we feel. Love is what we do—how we act and relate to others.[10]

While in verse 4 John talked about "walking in truth," in verse 6 he talks about "walking according to His commandments" (plural) and "walking in it." The closest antecedent of the pronoun "it" is "commandment," which refers to mutual love. What does this mean?

1. Christians walk in the truth; that is, they live the true life committed to God and His truth as revealed in Jesus Christ.
2. They walk in love, keeping the commandment to love each other.
3. Love motivates them to walk in all of God's commandments. " '*The* command' is that we should love one another, while 'the commands' are the detailed requirements which unfold the structure of this central command."[11]

Truth, love, and obedience to the commandments may have been "commodities in short supply in some section of the Johannine community" and had to "become top priorities."[12] Stott points out that "Christian liberty is not inconsistent with law any more than love is. True, Christians are not 'under law' in that our salvation does not depend on obedience to the law. Yet this does not relieve us of the obligation to keep the law. . . . The freedom with which Christ has made us free is not freedom to break the law, but freedom to keep it."[13]

III. Going Beyond the Teaching of Christ (2 John 7–9)

Verses 7–9 take us to the "deceivers," with their false understanding of Jesus. The situation seems to be the same as the one that we have already encountered in 1 John. The deceivers' views of Jesus differ radically from the apostles' teaching, and these secessionists propagate their positions. The situation has become so bad that many people have left the church and have become deceivers themselves.

In verse 7, the false teachers are characterized (1) as many, (2) as deceivers,

(3) as those who do not confess Jesus Christ's full humanity, (4) as those who have left the church, and (5) as antichrist. While at the beginning of verse 7 the deceivers appear in the plural, at the end of the same verse the singular is used and the term *antichrist* is added. Obviously, the deceivers prefigure the future antichrist. Johnson sees in the term *antichrist* a reference "to a figure of the end times, an apocalyptic character, like Paul's 'man of lawlessness.' . . . The Elder sees in these false teachers a harbinger of the end of this age."[14] Witherington writes, "It seems clear enough that a distinction is made between the final antichrist figure, who brings things to a climax and preliminary antichrist figures. . . . Our author neither fuses nor confuses the antichrists (plural) with the antichrist (singular) . . . , but he does see the former as foreshadowing the latter, who is still yet to come."[15]

While 1 John 4:2 notes that "Jesus Christ *has come* in the flesh," 2 John 7 remarks that "Jesus Christ *is coming* in the flesh," employing a present tense. The coming of Jesus can hardly refer to His second coming. It clearly deals with His incarnation "in the flesh." Yet this incarnation does not take place again in any moment of history. Rather, it happened once and its results remain. Jesus Christ has become flesh and remains flesh (continual present tense). Similar wording is used in John 6:14 and 11:27. John's message is that the incarnation of Jesus Christ has lasting effects. Akin talks about "the abiding reality of the incarnation."[16] Smalley holds that Jesus' incarnation and humanness is ongoing.[17] For John, "it was axiomatic that there had been a true incarnation, that the Word had become flesh and remained flesh."[18] Stott agrees: "The two natures, manhood and Godhead, were united already at his birth, never to be divided. The combination of the perfect and the present tenses (in 1 Jn. 4:2 and here) emphasizes this permanent union of natures in the one person."[19]

Verse 8 contains the second exhortation. Church members have to constantly beware to avoid being affected by the deceivers and thus losing their "full reward." Some Greek manuscripts read, "Watch out that you do not lose what *you* have worked for" instead of "what *we* have worked for." "You" is favored by the NIV and the RSV, while "we" is preferred by the majority of the older and newer English translations and the Modern Greek text.

The opinion of the expositors is also divided on what it means to lose the full reward. Some suggest that it has nothing to do with "winning or losing their salvation" but rather refers to "their reward for faithful service."[20] However, this interpretation seems to be based on the idea that true believers cannot fall away. New Testament scholars who do not subscribe to this view talk about the potential loss of one's salvation and connect the reward with eternal life as found in 1 John 5:11, 12.[21] The warning includes an indirect affirmation: If you do not follow the heretics, you can count on the reward that is a free gift from God.

According to verse 9, the secessionists have "run ahead" and gone too far. They "may think of themselves as 'progressives,' 'modern,' or philosophically and theologically 'up-to-date.' But to the Elder, they have left authentic Christianity and no longer have God."[22] This is true for all who have moved away from the biblical understanding of Jesus Christ. Stott says, "They had advanced so far that they had even left God behind them!"[23] But John is not opposed to a better understanding of biblical truth. He is opposed to those views that have no place for Jesus Christ or misinterpret the person and work of the Son of God. Such views are apostasy, not progress.

Teaching, mentioned twice in verse 9, may designate instruction given by a teacher or the content of what has been taught, whether orthodox or heretic. In our passage, it is the apostles' teaching about Jesus that is being challenged. Those who accept the biblical teaching and faithfully remain in it "have" the Father and the Son. The rejection of this teaching leads to a loss of one's relationship with the Father. No wonder John is convinced that doctrine matters. He warns us to watch out and not to go further than what Jesus and the apostles have taught. If believers heed this warning, they will experience the fulfillment of the promise at the end of verse 9: they will have both the Father and the Son.

IV. REFRAINING FROM HOSPITALITY? (2 JOHN 10, 11)

The Bible sees great value in hospitality, and it challenges Christians to be hospitable (Heb. 13:2; 1 Pet. 4:9). Jesus mingled with tax collectors, Pharisees, and others who may not always have had their theology or their lifestyle straight. How does such a call fit with what John is saying in 2 John 10, 11?

Although hospitality is a Christian virtue, there are limitations. If hospitality leads to directly or indirectly supporting false doctrines, it should be abandoned. In the first century A.D., teachers were traveling around, preaching in various places, and staying with church members, who would provide food and lodging. If such a teacher was propagating false doctrines, the hospitality provided would be understood as supporting his message. Church members wavering between the apostolic teaching and the new but false ideas—often proto-gnostic or later gnostic in nature—would be puzzled or would make wrong decisions if they saw a prominent church member or leader letting the deceiver stay with him or her.

The *Didache,* an early Christian writing, also deals with the problem of false teachers who disguised themselves as itinerant missionaries, and it points out how to relate to them: "Now, you should welcome anyone who comes your way and teaches you all we have been saying. But if the teacher proves himself renegade and by teaching contradicts all this, pay no attention to him. . . . Welcome every apostle on arriving, as if he were the Lord. But he must not stay beyond one day. In case of necessity, however, the next day too. If he stays three days, he is a false prophet. . . . If he asks for money, he is a false prophet."[24]

The last phrase of verse 10, repeated in the beginning of verse 11, deals with the church members' reaction to the false teacher. Some versions render the Greek phrase "not to give him a greeting" (NASB, ESV) or "not to greet him" (NKJV), while others use "not to welcome him" (NIV), and still others "not to bid him God speed" (KJV). Although "to greet" is a correct translation, the issue is not saying hello to these persons. "It meant to welcome, involving a show of acceptance and love and receptiveness. In fact, one could say that greeting someone as a brother or sister conveyed the impression that the person was a Christian in good standing."[25] Johnson adds, "*Anyone who welcomes him* . . . includes cooperation in and help with the mission of those who divided the community."[26] Akin suggests that the phrase functions as a farewell and "means something like 'God bless' or 'may it go well.' It is an expression of affirmation and support. John says there is to be no encouragement whatsoever. Showing hospitality or verbal agreement would be to participate in their evil work."[27]

John is not proposing that believers hate or have no concern for those holding erroneous views or that they avoid completely any contact with persons who think differently. He is saying that Christians must be aware of the fact that their behavior could be understood as an endorsement of ideas opposed to truth. If this is the case, they must be very careful.

It has been suggested that in verses 10 and 11, John is not so much concerned with the behavior of an individual believer but with that of the entire church and that the house mentioned in verse 10 is not a private dwelling place but the place where the church meets for worship. The church should not encourage a teacher who preaches heresy.[28] This may be correct, but it does not relieve us from our own individual responsibility.

Today, many have lost the sense of how problematic heresies can be and have become quite tolerant if not indifferent to biblical truth. They consider it judgmental or arrogant even to say that such a thing as heresy exists. The danger is that tolerance may become compromise, and compromise heresy. No church is immune to such a development. John reminds us that there is a basic difference between truth and error, that it matters what we believe, and that our beliefs affect our relationship with God.

V. COMMUNICATING WITH ONE ANOTHER (2 JOHN 12, 13)

Verses 12 and 13 form the conclusion of the letter. The elect lady (v. 1) has an elect sister (v. 13). The concept of joy found in verse 4 is repeated. The author wants his congregations to experience complete joy. The conclusion of 2 John allows us to see John's personal interest in his readers and his desire to meet with them personally. Although an oral presentation of a message has advantages, there are also advantages to written messages—such as careful crafting of the text, preservation of the communication, sharing it with others, and a fast response. Nevertheless, John hoped to see the believers face to face.

John wanted to communicate with his church members openly, to reaffirm them, and to warn them. Open and tactful communication is normally better than assuming that issues will disappear by themselves. It is better to solve a problem than not to touch it at all, and it is better to encourage each other than never to say an affirmative word.

The message that John communicates is quite strong. When it comes to antichrists, John leaves no room for negotiation or compromise. We are reminded of Paul's attitude when he wrote the letter to the Galatians (Gal. 1:6–9). John wants to protect churches and church members.

CONCLUSION

John's second letter portrays how the apostle cares for his church and longs that all members be strong in their faith. He encourages, exhorts, and warns the church members, stressing truth and love. Our life as Christians must exhibit the characteristics of walking in the truth, walking in love, and walking in God's commandments. Then, instead of being deceived, we will be able to help others.

"The apostle teaches that while we should manifest Christian courtesy, we are authorized to call sin and sinners by their right names—that this is consistent with true charity. While we are to love the souls for whom Christ died, and labor for their salvation, we should not make a compromise with sin. We are not to unite with the rebellious, and call this charity. God requires His people in this age of the world to stand, as did John in his time, unflinchingly for the right, in opposition to soul-destroying errors."[29]

CHAPTER 13

JOHN'S LETTER TO GAIUS (3 JOHN)

Because persons such as Alexander the Great, Napoleon, and Hitler became overly ambitious and greedy for power and possessions, they tried to establish huge empires, waging wars and killing multitudes of innocent people. Some did not even care for their own people. Others tried to establish economic or religious empires and thereby exploited, oppressed, and persecuted others. The saying "Power corrupts; absolute power corrupts absolutely" is oftentimes true. As tragic as this is, it is nothing new—the great controversy began with a power struggle in heaven.

As familiar as such power struggles are, it still is very sad to see such things going on in the Christian community, which is supposed to have a completely different value system built on the exemplary life and the teachings of Jesus. Third John reports such a power struggle in one of the early churches. On one side were the apostle John, Gaius, and Demetrius. On the other side was Diotrephes, who was trying to establish his supremacy.

The third letter of John shares common vocabulary with the other two letters, but it also differs from them. Jesus does not appear by name in 3 John. On the other hand, the term *church* shows up directly. While 1 and 2 John deal primarily with Christ, who had been misrepresented by false teachers, 3 John wrestles with a leadership crisis in a local church.

I. The Elder and Gaius (3 John 1–4, 13–15)

Third John is one of the few letters in the New Testament that is addressed to an individual person. Not only is it an extremely important witness about trends in the early churches toward the end of the first century A.D. that became more pronounced in the second century, but it also contains important lessons for Christianity today.

This letter is addressed to a certain Gaius, a positive character. Verses 1–8 deal with him. The letter moves on to Diotrephes, a negative character (vv. 9, 10), and concludes with Demetrius, another positive character (v. 12). Verse 11 forms a bridge between the negative and the positive examples. Verses 13–15 constitute a conclusion. Here is an outline of 3 John:

vv. 1–4	Introduction
v. 1	Sender and recipient
v. 2	A prayer wish
vv. 3, 4	A word of praise
vv. 5–12	Message
vv. 5–8	A. Commendation of Gaius's hospitality
vv. 9, 10	B. Condemnation of Diotrephes
vv. 11, 12	A'. Recommendation of Demetrius
vv. 13–15	Conclusion

The emphasis on love and truth was also found in 1 and 2 John and links the Johannine Epistles. There is also an important stress on ethical behavior. It occurs in words and phrases such as *to walk in the truth, to perform works,* and especially *to do/to act.*

v. 5	To do/act faithfully
v. 6	To do well
v. 10	To do with evil words
v. 11	To do good
v. 11	To do evil

Although John was an apostle, he calls himself "elder" (3 John 1). In addressing a group of elders, Peter had done the same, although, of course, he too was an apostle (see 1 Pet. 5:1). John may have followed this usage for a number of reasons, some of which do not necessarily exclude others: (1) He may have used this title to refer to his position, his age, or both. The latter use seems more probable. (2) By using the title *elder,* he may have been indicating that the letter was official communication. (3) The title may point to the respect and authority that was due to its holder. (4) His use of *elder* may point to his humility and collegiality, an attitude that differs widely from that of Diotrephes.

Acts 20:4 mentions a Gaius of Derbe, but we don't know whether or not this is the Gaius that John addresses in this letter. The apostle must have had a good relationship with Gaius. He calls him "beloved" (v. 2).

Gaius is a Roman name, so Gaius may have been a Gentile Christian who was wealthy enough to support and accommodate traveling missionaries. He may have been an important and well-respected person in the local church, although he probably was not the main leader.[1] The fact that John "is not writing to the leader of the congregation means that considerable trouble is brewing."[2]

Gaius was doing well spiritually; however, his health seems to have been poor (v. 2). John wished and prayed that Gaius would do well. Today we know that emotional, mental, or spiritual problems can cause physical suffering. On the other hand, physical sickness can lead to being depressed, a rebellious attitude against God, doubt, suicidal thoughts, and so on. If one aspect of our personality suffers, the others are also affected. Therefore, it is normally best if we enjoy complete health. For people today, the wish for physical health and wholeness must be joined with taking the responsibility to do something for one's well-being. However, there's no justification for using this verse as proof of a "prosperity gospel"—that is, that God's children will always enjoy wonderful health and an abundance of wealth.

John rejoiced that Gaius was walking in the truth and that fellow believers who had met Gaius praised his wonderful Christian attitude. On his part, John longed to meet Gaius and talk to him personally.

II. GAIUS AND HIS MINISTRY TO THE CHURCH (3 JOHN 5–8)

In his second letter, John had addressed the issue of hospitality and had warned against being hospitable to traveling "missionaries" who were teaching heresies about Jesus Christ. The church and true believers cannot support antichrists. In 3 John, the apostle comes back to the issue of hospitality. This time, he encourages Gaius to continue extending hospitality to true itinerant missionaries (v. 5), and he criticizes Diotrephes for refusing to receive these servants of the Lord and for building instead his own power basis (vv. 9, 10). Because of the complementary issues regarding hospitality, the two letters are best read together to get a balanced picture.

Third John stresses that the traveling missionaries needed help (vv. 5, 6, 8).

They were doing the work of God in preaching the gospel for free (v. 7), and they needed a place to stay overnight, food, and support for the continuation of their journeys. As a matter of policy, they should not become dependent on Gentiles (v. 7). "A Christian congregation supporting its minister is one thing; missionaries begging money from unbelievers is another."[3] By supporting the Lord's servants, church members "become fellow workers for the truth" (v. 8).

Third John is not about heretic missionaries; rather, it is concerned with missionaries who are dedicated to God and preaching sound doctrine. Gaius had supported them and had shown hospitality toward them. These missionaries must have been impressed and must have mentioned Gaius favorably in church. John not only praised Gaius for his kindness but also supported fully hospitality in cases in which heresy was not involved. The *we* in verse 8 stands in contrast to non-Christians, and it includes us today. The Bible calls all Christians to be hospitable at all times (Rom. 12:13; Heb. 13:2; 1 Pet. 4:9). We must take this call seriously.

III. THE MAN DIOTREPHES (3 JOHN 9, 10)

The term *to accept/to receive* marks the beginning and end of the discussion of the unacceptable behavior of Diotrephes:

A. What Diotrephes is doing: He does not receive John and his group.
    B. What John will do: He will call to attention Diotrephes' deeds.
A'. What Diotrephes is doing: He gossips maliciously about John and his church, refuses to welcome the brothers, and stops those who want to be hospitable.

After having pointed to Gaius and his ministry, John is now ready to tackle the problem of Diotrephes, the leader of the church. Diotrephes was hindering hospitality, and church members were even being disfellowshiped for supporting traveling missionaries (v. 10). "The irony here is that Diotrephes was prepared to treat the proper missionaries in the very way that the old man had instructed the congregation in 2 John to treat the heretics."[4]

Why would John share this information with Gaius? Did Gaius not know the problems himself? If Gaius and Diotrephes were members of the same church, there are two basic options, and they are not necessarily exclusive of each other: (1) Gaius may not have known much about the situation because he lived far from the church and his poor health did not allow him to attend the church regularly. (2) John may have written a previous letter to the church (v. 9) addressed to Diotrephes, who suppressed or even destroyed it because he did not like the content and was not willing to take directives from the apostle.[5] So John wrote another letter, 3 John, this time, however, addressing it to Gaius in the hope that he would share the letter with the church. John included information that Gaius was familiar with to some extent but that was important for the church to know. In this way, John let the church know that he was working on a solution. This scenario works whether or not Gaius knew Diotrephes' attitude.

Obviously, the situation was deteriorating rapidly. Not only were church members being pushed aside or even disfellowshiped for showing basic Christian courtesy to others, but apparently, Diotrephes was also trying to establish himself as the one who was in control of the congregation. He may have confused lust for power with zeal for the gospel. He arrogantly rejected the authority of the apostle John and others.

This was a dangerous development, because it seems as though Diotrephes wanted to be a kind of autocrat and wanted do be independent from those who were overseeing the church on a larger scale. Such an attitude had the potential of bringing dramatic change to the nature of the church and the role church members played in it. The problem was not theology. Most probably, John and Diotrephes agreed on the doctrines. The issue was power. Therefore, Stott indicates that the issue was a moral problem and had to do with sin.[6] John says Diotrephes is wrong in six ways:[7] (1) He loves to be first. (2) He does not want to have anything to do with John and his group and does not accept John. (3) With wicked words, he brings false charges against John. (4) He refuses to welcome the brothers. (5) He hinders those who are willing to care for traveling missionaries. (6) He excommunicates these brothers from church.

"Self-love vitiates all relationships. Diotrephes slandered John, cold-shouldered the missionaries and excommunicated the loyal believers—all because he loved himself and wanted to have preeminence. Personal vanity still lies at the root of most dissensions in every local church today."[8]

IV. The Testimony About Demetrius (3 John 11, 12)

Why does John write verse 11 to Gaius, whom he praises for his walk in the truth? It could very well be that Diotrephes had the majority of the church members on his side. In such a situation, it is not easy to steer a clear course and not be affected by others. One can easily feel that the majority must be right and something must be wrong with oneself. In any case, Gaius is encouraged to imitate the good, which so far he has done. "The verse is thus basically an appeal to Gaius not to be misled by Diotrephes and to follow his example."[9]

Verse 11 is a transitional statement that builds a bridge between what John has said about Diotrephes and what he is going to say about Demetrius. Evil has a representative in the arrogant and ambitious leader Diotrephes. On the other hand, Demetrius is a good example for Gaius to follow, as is the apostle John. The latter establishes in verse 11 that unloving conduct and an evil attitude call into question a person's claim to be a follower of Christ. You cannot do evil and claim to be "of God."

A. Beloved, do not imitate what is **evil**
  B. but what is ***good.***
  B'. He who ***does good*** is of God.
A'. He who **does evil** has not seen God.

There is a Demetrius in Acts 19:23–29, a silversmith who was responsible for the riot in Ephesus when Paul preached the gospel there. Nothing indicates that this is the same person that John mentions. The name Demas may be derived from Demetrius. And a man named Demas is mentioned in Colossians 4:14; 2 Timothy 4:10; and Philemon 1:24. He was one of Paul's fellow workers but deserted him because "he loved this present world." Again, there is no indication that this Demas was the Demetrius of 3 John 12.

We do know that Demetrius was a Gentile Christian. His name referred to the Greek god Demeter. Demetrius supported the apostle John and may have been one of his associates and one of the traveling missionaries. He was orthodox and had "a threefold testimony to his character"[10]—namely, from everyone, from the truth, and from John himself. "Truth" seems to be personified here.

John may have planned to confront Diotrephes, and he may have wanted Demetrius to be present when he did so. Scholars seem to agree that Demetrius was the letter bearer.[11] He may have prepared the way for the apostle by carrying the letter to Gaius, who in turn may have informed at least some of the church members.

Because of the difficult situation in the church, Gaius and other church members may have had reservations against welcoming Demetrius to their home. They knew Diotrephes would give them a hard time. So it may have been Gaius's task to grant Demetrius hospitality.

V. LEADERSHIP CRISIS IN THE EARLY CHURCH (3 JOHN 6, 9, 10)

At the end of the first century A.D., most of the eyewitnesses to Jesus, including most of the twelve apostles, had passed away. New and less prestigious leaders had to take over. In such a situation, crises can easily arise. According to this letter, the problem John was addressing was not so much theology but rather personal ambition and possibly an attempt to change the way churches were governed. Yet in the long run, the biblical doctrine of the church would be affected.

Some commentators suggest that the monarchical episcopate "was already being introduced."[12] However that may be, "by AD 115, when Bishop Ignatius of Antioch wrote his letter to the Asian churches, 'monarchical episcopacy' (the acceptance of a single bishop with authority over a group of presbyters) was established among them."[13] During New Testament times, the terms *elder* and *bishop* were used interchangeably (Acts 20:17, 28). At that time, a body or council of elders had developed (1 Tim. 4:14), indicating that decision-making was not left to any individual alone. Later, this changed dramatically. Bishops gained more and more power, eventually ruling like a monarch. A strict hierarchy was created, and the church became more or less identical with the so-called clergy, while the laity became unimportant. The ecclesiastical hierarchy reached its peak in the Middle Ages, with the pope as sole ruler of Christianity—with even greater authority than that held by kings and emperors.

According to the New Testament, all believers are part of the royal priesthood (1 Pet. 2:9; Rev. 1:5, 6). All have received spiritual gifts that are necessary for the church (1 Cor. 12:7, 27–31). Distinction between laity and clergy is foreign to the New Testament. All believers are the body of Christ. However, God has called some people to leadership positions in the church (1 Tim. 3:1–7) and has gifted them for the task. These persons should be respected (Heb. 13:7, 17). Leaders are not infallible and should not pretend to be so. In some cases, there may even be justified reasons for complaints (1 Tim. 5:19). If the leader must be confronted, it should be done carefully and lovingly. Leaders must indeed lead out, but they also need to be shepherds, and most of all, they need to be examples for the rest of the body of Christ. They must equip the church members to perform the ministry to which they are called (Eph. 4:11, 12). Qualifications for leaders are listed in both the Old Testament and the New Testament.

Summarizing, one can say that the New Testament is opposed to chaos and anarchy in the church. It mentions leadership for the local level as well as the universal church. However, Jesus Himself stressed that leadership in the church/churches must be servant leadership (Mark 10:42–44). A group of elders rather than one person alone governed local churches. Decision-making involved the entire church or representatives of the church (Acts 6:1–7; 15:6, 22–25).

Christians are challenged to use a model of church governance that reflects New Testament principles. They must avoid allowing church leadership or the church as a whole to become a mere copy of the political system of the country in which the church is located. They must also avoid power struggles and kingly rule as depicted in 3 John and instead encourage members to work together as brothers and sisters and ambassadors of Christ, following His example.[14]

"God has not set any kingly power in the Seventh-day Adventist church to control the whole body or to control any branch of the work. He has not provided that the burden of leadership shall rest upon a few men. Responsibilities are distributed among a large number of competent men."[15]

> The work is great, and there is no one human mind that can plan for the work which needs to be done. . . .
>
> Now I want to say, God has not put any kingly power in our ranks to control this or that branch of the work.[16]

The apostle concludes 3 John in a way similar to his conclusion of 2 John (which may indicate that the letters were written at the same time).[17] The Greek text has 15 verses in 3 John. Some English translations, such as the KJV, the NKJV, and the NIV, have merged the Greek verses 14 and 15 into one verse and therefore contain only 14 verses. Others, such as the NASB, the ESV, and the RSV, follow the Greek text and therefore have three verses concluding 3 John.

John knows that his letter is not sufficient. The ending of 3 John contains a greater sense of urgency than does the conclusion of 2 John. John knows he must come very soon and hopes to be able to talk to Gaius face to face. John's wish that Gaius may have peace is very appropriate. Especially in all the turmoil that Gaius and those who side with the apostle find themselves, the peace of God is important.

CONCLUSION

Witherington notes, "What these letters . . . show is that there was genuine concern for orthodoxy and orthopraxy near the end of the first century in the Johannine community. These documents are brutally honest about the flaws in the churches, which speaks well for the honesty of our writer." "There is much we could learn from these practical documents that too often are neglected because of their brevity or location toward the end of the canon. We could learn much about the importance of truth, the need for leadership, the ways a Christian should handle a crisis, how establishing social networks and loving relationships and generous hospitality is imperative, and how Christian leaders should go around persuading their flocks."[18]

To state this in terms of the content of 3 John: All of us exert an influence. This influence can be either detrimental or beneficial. We can either be a Gaius or Demetrius who labors for the kingdom of God or a Diotrephes who hinders God's cause and becomes a stumbling block for others. Third John calls us to be like Gaius and Demetrius, furthering the work of God and becoming blessings to many. The apostle is convinced that "right will win out. Such confidence should characterize all who live their lives under 'the Name.' "[19]

Endnotes

Chapter 1: Jesus and the Johannine Letters

1. Compare D. A. Carson, D. J. Moo, L. Morris, *An Introduction to the New Testament* (Grand Rapids, Mich.: Zondervan Publishing House, 1992), 446, 447; Francis D. Nichol, ed., *The Seventh-day Adventist Bible Commentary* (Washington, D.C.: Review and Herald® Publishing Association, 1957), 7:625.

2. John Drane, *Introducing the New Testament* (Minneapolis, Minn.: Fortress Press, 2001), 452.

3. Compare Klaus Wengst, *Der erste, zweite und dritte Brief des Johannes,* Ökumenischer Taschenbuch-Kommentar zum Neuen Testament 16 (Gütersloh: Gütersloher Verlagshaus Gerd Mohn, 1978), 25, 26.

4. Compare ibid., 684, who mentions both options.

5. Compare Carson, 451; Drane, 451.

6. Compare Donald Guthrie, *Hebrews.* Tyndale New Testament Commentaries, rev. ed. (Grand Rapids, Mich.: William B. Eerdmans Publishing, 1990), 883, 884; Nichol, 7:625.

7. However, two different Greek words are used.

8. Compare Drane, 453.

9. Stephen S. Smalley, *1, 2, 3 John,* Word Biblical Commentary 51 (Waco, Tex.: Word Publishers, 1984), xxxiii, xxxiv.

10. Compare I. Howard Marshall, *The Epistles of John,* New International Commentary on the New Testament (Grand Rapids, Mich.: William B. Eerdmans Publishing, 1978), 22–24.

11. Abraham Terian, "First John: Light, Love and Fellowship," *Advent-*

ist Review, December 5, 1985, 6.
12. Terian, 6.
13. Carson, 455.

CHAPTER 2: EXPERIENCING THE WORD OF LIFE (1 JOHN 1:1–4)

1. Compare Daniel L. Akin, *1, 2, 3 John,* The New American Commentary (Nashville, Tenn.: Broadman and Holman Publishers, 2001), 51; Ben Witherington III, *Letters and Homilies for Hellenized Christians, Volume I: A Socio-Rhetorical Commentary on Titus, 1–2 Timothy and 1–3 John* (Downers Grove, Ill.: InterVarsity Press, 2007), 440.
2. Raymond E. Brown, *The Gospel According to John 1–12,* The Anchor Bible 29A (New York: Doubleday, 1966), 154.
3. Akin, 55.
4. Witherington, 443.
5. Compare Thomas F. Johnson, *1, 2, and 3 John,* New International Biblical Commentary (Peabody, Mass.: Hendrickson Publishers, 1993), 27; John R. W. Stott, *The Letters of John: An Introduction and Commentary,* Tyndale New Testament Commentaries (Grand Rapids, Mich.: William B. Eerdmans Publishing, 1988), 27, 28.
6. Stott, 65.
7. Stott, 71.
8. Witherington, 445.
9. Stott, 68.
10. Smalley, 12.
11. Stott, 69.

CHAPTER 3: TURNING AWAY FROM SIN (1 JOHN 1:5–2:2)

1. Johnson, 28.
2. Stott, 75.
3. Compare Johnson, 29.
4. Witherington, 451.
5. Compare Akin, 71.
6. Witherington, 450.
7. Compare Smalley, 24, 29; Witherington, 455.
8. Nichol, 7:632.
9. Stott, 84.
10. Johnson, 33.
11. Johnson, 31.
12. Compare Nichol, 7:631.
13. Stott, 80.
14. Witherington, 454.
15. Stott, 83.
16. Compare Stott, 84.
17. Johnson, 34.
18. Compare Smalley, 37; Stott, 86; Witherington, 459.
19. Related terms are *hilastērion* ("propitiation," "expiation"—for example, Rom. 3:24) and *hilaskomai* ("to bring about forgiveness," "to make propitiation"—for example, Heb. 2:17).
20. Witherington, 460.
21. See, by way of example, Akin, 82–85; I. Howard Marshall, *The Epistles of John,* New International Commentary on the New Testament (Grand Rapids, Mich.: William B.

Eerdmans Publishing, 1990), 118; Stott, 87–93; Witherington, 460–465

22. Stott, 93.

23. Compare Brown's lengthy discussion (217–222); Smalley, 38–40.

24. Ellen G. White, *The Acts of the Apostles* (Mountain View, Calif.: Pacific Press® Publishing Association, 1963), 561, 565.

CHAPTER 4: KEEPING HIS COMMANDMENTS (1 JOHN 2:3–11)

1. Wilma Ann Bailey, *"You Shall Not Kill" or "You Shall Not Murder"? The Assault on a Biblical Text* (Collegeville, Tenn.: Liturgical Press, 2005).
2. Bailey, 52.
3. Compare Witherington, 466.
4. Compare Stott, 94.
5. Compare Marshall, 121.
6. Akin, 90, 91.
7. Johnson, 40.
8. Witherington, 466.
9. Smalley, 45, 46.
10. Compare Wengst, 67.
11. Smalley, 49.
12. John 14 contains a similar sequence: (1) keeping Jesus' commandments (vv. 15, 21) and (2) keeping His words (vv. 23, 24).
13. Marshall, 127.
14. Johnson, 42.
15. Stott, 97.
16. Marshall, 128.
17. Ibid., 128, 129.
18. Witherington, 472.
19. See Akin, 96, and Smalley, 56.
20. Stott, 99.
21. See Wengst, 77.
22. Stott, 98; compare Johnson, 43.
23. Compare Johnson, 44, 45; Smalley, 62.
24. Painter, 170.

CHAPTER 5: RENOUNCING WORLDLINESS (1 JOHN 2:12–17)

1. Peters, *The Stem Cell Debate* (Minneapolis, Minn.: Fortress Press, 2007), 58.
2. These are the *Novum Testamentum Graece* by Nestle-Aland and the United Bible Society's *Greek New Testament.*
3. D. Moody Smith, *First, Second, and Third John,* Interpretation (Louisville, Ky.: John Knox Press, 1991), 63.
4. G. Sherman and J. C. Tuggy, *A Semantic and Structural Analysis of the Johannine Epistles* (Dallas, Tex.: Summer Institute of Linguistics, 1994), 41.
5. Brown, 300.
6. Witherington, 476; compare Marshall, 138.
7. Compare Akin, 105; Johnson, 50; Marshall, 139, 140; Smalley, 73, 74; and Witherington, 476. Stott, 102, understands it as a reference to God the Father.
8. J. I. Packer, *Knowing God* (Downers Grove, Ill.: InterVarsity

Press, 1973), 25, 26, 27–31, 33, 34.

9. Akin, 107.

10. Compare Akin, 106.

11. Smalley, 80.

12. C. H. Dodd, *The Johannine Epistles,* Moffat New Testament Commentary (London: Hodder & Stoughton, 1946), 39.

13. Johnson, 52.

14. Dodd, 46.

15. Johnson, 53.

16. Marshall, 144, 145. Akin, 110, talks about overeating and drunkenness.

17. Witherington, 478.

18. Smalley, 84.

19. William R. G. Loader, *The Johannine Epistles* (London: Epworth, 1992), 25.

20. Akin, 111.

21. R. A. Culpepper, *1, 2, 3 John,* Knox Preaching Guides (Atlanta, Ga.: John Knox, 1985), 41.

22. Dick Rentfro, "On Temporary Assignment," *Adventist Review,* June 26, 2008.

CHAPTER 6: REJECTING ANTICHRISTS (1 JOHN 2:18–29; 4:1–6)

1. For example, David E. Aune, *Revelation 6–16,* Word Biblical Commentary (Nashville, Tenn.: Thomas Nelson Publishers, 1998), 752; G. K. Beale, *The Book of Revelation,* The New International Greek Testament Commentary (Grand Rapids, Mich.: William B. Eerdmans, 1999), 686; Grant R. Osborne, *Revelation,* Baker Exegetical Commentary on the New Testament (Grand Rapids, Mich.: Baker Academic, 2002), 495.

2. Smalley, 93.

3. Witherington, 484, 485.

4. Stott, 114. For an extensive discussion, see pages 112–114.

5. For instance, the word *legō* means "to say," "to speak," or "to tell." But *antilegō* means "to oppose," "to object," or "to contradict" (Titus 1:9; Luke 2:34).

6. Stott, 109–110. Compare Johnson, 59.

7. Marshall, 151. Compare Witherington, 485.

8. Johnson, 57.

9. Marshall, 122.

10. Johnson, 59.

11. Marshall, 204, suggests, "The word 'spirit' here must mean either 'utterance inspired by a spirit' or 'person inspired by a spirit.' In the latter case the thought is perhaps of the individual spirit of a prophet, which might be inspired by God or Satan."

12. Compare Smalley, 224.

13. Johnson, 98.

14. Walter A. Elwell, ed., *Evangelical Dictionary of Theology* (Grand Rapids, Mich.: Baker Book House, 1984), 326.

15. Marshall, 208.

16. Compare Marshall, 153; Stott, 111.

17. The last phrase of verse 27 can be translated "remain in him" or "you remain in him." However, the very same phrase in the next verse must be translated as an imperative. Therefore, it is very likely that the last phrase of verse 17 is an imperative too.
18. Johnson, 60.
19. Stott, 117, 118.

CHAPTER 7: LIVING AS CHILDREN OF GOD (1 JOHN 3:1–10)

1. Akin, 132, 133.
2. Stott, 122.
3. Johnson, 68.
4. Smalley, 146.
5. Witherington, 497.
6. Marshall, 172.
7. Compare Johnson, 68.
8. Compare Grayston, 104.
9. Akin, 138.
10. H. H. Hobbs, *The Epistles of John* (Nashville, Tenn.: Thomas Nelson Publishers, 1983), 81.
11. Akin, 140.
12. Compare Marshall, 176, 177.
13. See Witherington, 499.
14. Stott, 126.
15. Compare Akin, 141, 147; Smalley, 156; Witherington, 501.
16. George Reid and Ekkehardt Mueller, "Christ's Death and Our Salvation," *Reflections: A BRI Newsletter,* July 2008, 6.
17. Witherington, 500.
18. Compare John 8:46; Acts 3:14; 2 Cor. 5:21; Heb. 4:15; 7:26; 1 Pet. 1:19; 2:21, 22.
19. Akin, 142.
20. Witherington, 500.
21. See Stott, 135–140.
22. Akin, 143.
23. Compare Akin, 143; Johnson, 71, 74; Stott, 131.
24. Grayston, 107.
25. Compare Johnson, 74.
26. Compare Akin, 149; Smalley, 174.

CHAPTER 8: LOVING BROTHERS AND SISTERS (1 JOHN 3:11–24; 4:7–5:4)

1. Witherington, 497.
2. Marshall, 188.
3. Marshall, 190.
4. J. Denney, *The Death of Christ* (London: Tyndale Press, 1951), 103.
5. Marshall, 213.
6. Stott, 163.
7. Ibid.
8. Witherington, 531.
9. This is the meaning of "only begotten." "While there are many 'children of God,' there is only one 'Son of God.' " Johnson, 103.
10. Stott, 166, 167.
11. Marshall, 194, and 195, 196.
12. Compare Grayston, 115, 116. Akin, 164–166, expresses the idea more gently but seems to come to the same conclusion.
13. Grayston, 116.
14. Johnson, 88.

15. Ibid.
16. Smith, 97.
17. Stott, 172.
18. The phrase "keep the commandments" occurs also in John 14:15; 15:10 and in Revelation 12:17; 14:12, where it is used of the end-time remnant.
19. Stott, 155.
20. Stott, 176.
21. Marshall, 200.

CHAPTER 9: BELIEVING IN THE SON OF GOD (1 JOHN 5:1–12)

1. Heinz Zahrnt, *Warum ich glaube: Meine Sache mit God* (München: R. Piper & Company, 1977), 120–152.
2. For instance, ESV, NIV, and RSV translate similarly.
3. Stott, 175.
4. Johnson, 119, 120.
5. Stott, 176.
6. Marshall, 229.
7. Stott, 177.
8. Johnson, 125, mentions the different readings of verse 6 before affirming "by water and blood."
9. Compare Akin, 195–197; Johnson, 125, 126; Stott, 179–181.
10. Witherington, 545, suggests a modified position. He understands water as referring to Jesus' birth and blood as describing His death, pointing out that "water was used as a euphemism in Jewish literature to refer to (1) semen; (2) the fluid in which the fetus was floating; (3) the 'breaking of the waters' as the birth process started."
11. Marshall, 234.
12. Johnson, 128, suggests that John 5:31–47 should be seen behind this passage and as its background, because in this chapter, Jesus deals with valid testimony.
13. Compare Marshall, 240.
14. Stott, 185.
15. Stott, 182, 183. For a more extensive discussion, see Akin, 198–200; Brown, 775–787; and Marshall, 235–237.
16. Nichol, 7:675.

CHAPTER 10: CONFIDENCE (1 JOHN 5:13–21)

1. Stott, 187.
2. Johnson, 133.
3. Marshall, 244.
4. Johnson, 135.
5. Ellen G. White, *Steps to Christ* (Mountain View, Calif.: Pacific Press® Publishing Association, 1956), 51.
6. Stott, 188.
7. Witherington , 553.
8. Witherington, 551.
9. For a more detailed discussion see, for instance, Akin, 208–210; Stott, 189–191.
10. Akin, 208, 209.
11. Marshall, 248.
12. Stott, 191.
13. For instance, Akin, 210; Brown, 618; Johnson, 137; and Witherington, 551.

14. Akin, 210; Stott, 190–192.
15. For instance, Marshall, 249.
16. Marshall, 250.
17. Marshall, 249, 250; Smalley, 299; Witherington, 552–555.
18. Witherington, 555.
19. For instance, Akin, 212; Johnson, 138; Marshall, 252; Stott, 194, 195; Witherington, 559.
20. Compare Stott, 194.
21. Compare the verb "to be born" in John 18:37, where Jesus Himself employs it to point to His incarnation.
22. Johnson, 138; compare Stott, 194.
23. Akin, 212.
24. Loader, 78, 79.
25. Johnson, 138.
26. Stott, 195, 196.
27. For example, Stott, 197, 198.
28. For example, Akin, 214, 215; Johnson, 140, 141; Marshall, 254, 255; Witherington, 560, 561.
29. Compare Johnson, 140. Witherington, 560, sees the Son even in the first reference to the "True One": Jesus has come and has given us insight so that we understand Him to some extent.
30. Stott, 197.
31. Johnson, 141.
32. Compare Rudolf Schnackenburg, *Johannine Epistles* (New York: Crossroad, 1992), 263.
33. Witherington, 561.

CHAPTER 11: IMPORTANT THEMES IN 1 JOHN

1. Frank Thielman, *Theology of the New Testament: A Canonical and Synthetic Approach* (Grand Rapids, Mich.: Zondervan, 2005), 544.
2. Thielman, 551. While it is true that the death of Jesus included the fulfillment of the antitypical sacrifice that was offered on the Day of Atonement, the goat for the Lord (Lev. 16), it also fulfilled the daily service when in the evening and in the morning a lamb was slaughtered (Exod. 29:38–43). John 1:29 points to the Lamb (*amnos*) that takes away the sins of the world, and Revelation focuses on the Lamb (*arnion*) as the primary Christological title.
3. Frank J. Matera, *New Testament Theology: Exploring Diversity and Unity* (Louisville, Ky.: Westminster John Knox Press, 2007), 321, 322.
4. Compare Donald Guthrie, *New Testament Theology* (Downers Grove, Ill.: InterVarsity Press, 1981), 731.
5. Judith Lieu, *The Theology of the Johannine Epistles,* New Testament Theology (Cambridge: Cambridge University Press, 1991), 114.
6. Lieu, 117. We would understand such tradition as biblical tradition.
7. George Eldon Ladd, *A Theology of the New Testament* (Grand Rapids, Mich.: William B. Eerdmans Publishing, 1974), 613.
8. Ladd, 614.

9. Thielman, 547–549.
10. Guthrie, 933.
11. Lieu, 118.
12. Matera, 327.
13. See, for example, Ephesians 4:25–5:21.
14. Guthrie, 932.
15. Matera, 332.
16. Guthrie, 932.
17. Compare Thielman, 554.
18. Lieu, 28.
19. Ladd, 613.
20. Compare Ladd, 613.

CHAPTER 12: JOHN'S LETTER TO THE CHOSEN LADY (2 JOHN)

1. However, her sister mentioned in verse 13 would carry the very same name, which makes this option very improbable.
2. For a discussion of various positions, see Stott, 203, 204. The last options he calls "pure conjecture" (203).
3. Marshall, 60, 61.
4. Johnson, 147.
5. Marshall, 60.
6. Marshall, 61.
7. Stott, 207.
8. Witherington, 568.
9. Witherington, 569.
10. Stott, 209, notes, "Christian love belongs rather to the sphere of action than of emotion."
11. Marshall, 67.
12. Johnson, 154.
13. Stott, 210.
14. Johnson, 156; compare Stott, 212.
15. Witherington, 573, 574.
16. Akin, 229.
17. Smalley, 328, 329; compare Marshall, 70.
18. Marshall, 71.
19. Stott, 212.
20. Stott, 213.
21. See, for instance, Nichol 7:688; Johnson, 157.
22. Johnson, 157.
23. Stott, 213.
24. Didache 11:1, 2, 4–6.
25. Witherington, 579; compare Marshall, 74.
26. Johnson, 159.
27. Akin, 233.
28. Compare Witherington, 577, 578.
29. Ellen G. White, *The Sanctified Life* (Washington, D.C.: Review and Herald® Publishing Association, 1956), 65.

CHAPTER 13: JOHN'S LETTER TO GAIUS (3 JOHN)

1. This is true if Gaius and Diotrephes attend the same church. Johnson, 175, challenges this view, assuming that Gaius must be a member of another church, because John informs him what Diotrephes is doing. Stott, 228, opts for the same church.
2. Witherington, 586.

3. Stott, 227. He points out that devotees of various religions customarily collected money from the public.

4. Witherington, 593.

5. It is not likely that this letter was 1 John or 2 John because both of these letters were dealing with the Christological heresy, which may not have been an issue at all in 3 John. On the other hand, 1 and 2 John are not dealing with hospitality toward traveling missionaries as 3 John is. Compare Stott, 228, 229.

6. Stott, 230.

7. Compare Johnson, 175.

8. Stott, 231.

9. Marshall, 92.

10. Marshall, 93.

11. Compare Johnson, 180; Marshall, 93; Witherington, 594.

12. Stott, 230.

13. Ibid.

14. See also John 13:1–12; Eph. 4:11–16; 1 Thess. 5:12, 13; 1 Tim. 1:3, 4; 4:13; 5:22; Titus 1–3; 1 Pet. 5:1–4.

15. Ellen G. White, *Testimonies for the Church* (Mountain View, Calif.: Pacific Press®, 1948), 8:236.

16. Ellen G. White, *Last Day Events* (Boise, Idaho: Pacific Press®, 1992), 53.

17. Compare Johnson, 182.

18. Witherington, 596, 598.

19. Akin, 252.